OUTSTANDING
BLACK SERMONS

VOLUME 4

EDITED BY WALTER S. THOMAS

To: Lady C. Killmar
A great sister in Christ
God Bless
James W. ___
3/8/07
www.GreaterChristChurch.org

JUDSON PRESS
VALLEY FORGE

Outstanding Black Sermons, Volume 4
© 2001 by Judson Press, Valley Forge, PA 19482-0851
All rights reserved.

Unless otherwise indicated, Bible quotations in each chapter are
from the version cited in the chapter opener.
Scripture references marked KJV are from *The Holy Bible*, King James Version.
Scripture references marked NIV are taken from HOLY BIBLE:
New International Version, copyright © 1973, 1978, 1984.
Used by permission of Zondervan Bible Publishers.
Scripture quotations marked TLB are from *The Living Bible*, copyright © 1971.
Used by permission of Tyndale House Publishers, Inc., Wheaton, IL 60189.
All rights reserved.

Library of Congress Cataloging-in-Publication Data
Revised for volume 4.
Main entry under title:
Outstanding Black sermons.
Vol. 4 edited by Walter S. Thomas.
Includes bibliographical references.
1. Sermons, American—Afro-American.
I. Smith, J. Alfred (James Alfred) II. Hoard, Walter B.
III. Owens, Milton E. IV. Thomas, Walter S.
BV4241.5.09   252'.08996073   76-2084
ISBN 0-8170-0664-8 (vol. 1)   ISBN 0-8170-0832-2 (vol. 2)
ISBN 0-8170-0973-6 (vol. 3)   ISBN 0-8170-1378-4 (vol. 4)

Printed in the U.S.A.

07 06 05 04 03 02 01

10 9 8 7 6 5 4 3 2 1

*This book is dedicated
to all the sons and daughters
of New Psalmist Baptist Church,
who have been taught to give God
the best that they have
and to present Christ as Lord of all.
May you forever preach with power.*

CONTENTS

ACKNOWLEDGMENTS

I want to thank Judson Press for giving me the opportunity to work with this project. The preachers in this work are diverse, and being able to share with them and to present the messages that they preach is a blessing beyond measure. This work never would have been completed without the aid and assistance of my executive assistant, Odell Dickerson, who kept the project organized for completion. For over twenty years, the proofreading and typing of manuscripts has been the work of the most faithful administrator that any pastor can have. Mrs. Clara Major put this work together and ensured the manuscripts were presented in the proper form. Special thanks to Ms. Carla Pierce for typing and final editing of the project.

I would like to thank the church that I pastor, New Psalmist Baptist Church, for giving me the time to bring this project to fruition. I know that the inspiration that I receive from my family is part of the fire that fueled my passion for this kind of effort. Their encouragement to be the best preacher that I can be has always made me want to preach better and to know preachers who take preaching seriously.

Finally, I thank God for allowing me to be a part of the greatest workforce known to humanity. I thank God every day for making me a preacher. This is the work that each of us knows God has ordained us to do, and to do it in an outstanding way.

INTRODUCTION

Preaching is the vehicle that God has chosen to introduce the world to a saving faith. Paul, in his letter to the church at Rome, declared, "faith comes by hearing, and hearing by the word of God" (Romans 10:17). Why God has chosen this vehicle we will never know; but what is known is that preaching has changed the lives of countless thousands and brought them into fellowship with God. The central theme of preaching has been, and forever will be, that through the life, death, and resurrection of Jesus Christ, God has been revealed to humankind and has made a way for all of us to be reconciled back to God. This is the essence of the gospel, the substance of biblical preaching, and the hope of our calling.

The African American preacher has been called to present this Christ to a people who have been oppressed, and in many ways still are. From the dehumanizing practices of the antebellum South to the violence of the contemporary urban community, the preacher has had to present Christ as one who speaks to persons with these kinds of issues. For the African American preacher, there has never been the luxury of preaching just about one's personal morality, for the social predicaments demanded that the preacher address them first and offer some answers from God. The preacher has been both moral theologian and social prophet. In fact, this has been the hallmark of the African

American pulpit: never has it lost sight of the world in which people struggle with their salvation, their sin, and their relationship with God. In the words of the social scientists, the African American pulpit has understood the balance between the "nature and nurture" arguments.

Many traditions emphasize the moral life of the individual and hammer away at the thought that we are "born in sin." The African American preacher has never been light on sin. There is an awesome awareness of this dreaded force that destroys life and ruptures relationships. Yet, there always has been an appreciation for the "nurture issues," the "...shaped in iniquity" problem. The social context, with its institutional and systemic evils, has aided in the corruption of the soul and is an impediment that must be overcome. Not only must sin be killed in the person, but the system that harbors it and fosters it also must be exposed as flawed and fleeting. The gospel of Jesus does just that—it takes double aim on both the system and the soul and fires the Word of God deep into their cores.

This fourth volume of *Outstanding Black Sermons* brings together some of the best preachers in the pulpit today. These are millennium preachers—men and women who can speak powerfully to this generation. As you read these messages, you will discern the thread of continuity that defies age, gender, and denomination. The messages in this book come from persons who take preaching seriously and who are committed to the proclamation of the gospel. Some of the preachers included in this work have been preaching on the national circuit for quite a long time, while others are in the morning of a glorious ministry.

As you make yourself at home with this work, let the spirit of Christ speak to your heart and revive the flame of faith. This work does not seek to showcase major preachers; rather it seeks to showcase Christ, who is preached in a major way.

1

WASHBASIN RELIGION

CLAUDE R. ALEXANDER JR.

JOHN 13:1-17

The image of Jesus washing the feet of the disciples is one of the most striking images within the Gospels. The very portrait of the Word made flesh, the image of the invisible God and the fullness of the Godhead bodily bending down with a towel around his waist and cleaning the feet of sinful men is one that turns the sensibilities of the world upside down. The sentiment of the world is that we are to strive to be on top, to be the best, and to be number one. The sensibility of the world says that we've made it when we move from the background to the foreground, from the sideline to the field of play, and from backstage to front and center stage. The world intimates that progress in life is measured by the move from obscurity to prominence and from servitude to autonomy, if not sovereignty. Yes, the world suggests that we prize a transition from back tables and side tables to head tables. Yet, we have this picture of Jesus leaving the table, taking up a towel and washbasin, and washing the feet of the disciples. Jesus even takes it one step further by stating that such an action is the pathway to blessing. In so doing, Jesus asserts that his followers must adopt a washbasin religion.

This image of Jesus is stunning, especially when you consider the fact that it was conducted impromptu. Jesus did not do like many of us when we conduct foot washing services. We announce the services at least one day in advance, hoping that people will wash their feet before they come to service. Jesus gave no prior warning. He just began to wash the soiled, sweaty, and smelly feet of his disciples. These were the feet of grown men. They were hard and callused. The sizes were at least nine and above. The dirt from the first disciple's feet was enough to fill the basin. Yet, Jesus washed all twelve pair. He declares that we are to do likewise.

If that weren't arresting enough, the mere consideration of the men whose feet the Lord washes is startling. The identities of the persons are enough to send you out. There is Judas, whom John identifies as being one whom the devil entices to betray Jesus. Here is one who is under satanic influence. He is under satanic influence to harm Jesus. Jesus suggests that we give of ourselves in humble service in the midst of those who are under satanic influence. Serving Christ places us in direct contact with those who are influenced by the devil. You see them every day. They are in the workplace. Some may even exist in the circles of family and friends. They are those who make themselves available for the adversary's usage to bring discomfort, distress, and dis-ease in your immediate environment. Yet, Jesus, by way of his example, instructs us to take up the towel and humbly serve.

Not only is Judas among those whose feet Jesus washes, Simon Peter is also present. He is the one who will deny Jesus thrice in just a few hours. He is one whose lack of courage will cause him to shrink from his stance of faith and loyalty to the cause of Christ. In short, he is scared. Jesus places the pathway to blessing within the parameters of washing the feet of the scared. You know the scared. They are those who are loud and boisterous during times of ease and prosperity. However, when things are not as easy, or as popular, they shrink from view. When put to the test during moments of trial and adversity, the audacity wanes. Like the lion in the *Wizard of Oz*, they need courage. We are not only called to serve in the midst of the satanically influenced, but also to serve in the midst of the selfish. The remaining ten will leave Jesus in a few hours due to their concerns about themselves.

Yes, this is an extraordinary occurrence, but it is also the expectation placed upon us. I must admit that the satanically influenced, the scared, and the selfish aren't the most appealing categories and environments. The last thing that comes to mind at the mentioning of them is washing their feet or serving them in a sacrificial and self-denying manner. Nevertheless, it is the illustration that Jesus uses as being the pathway to blessing. It is one that raises the singular question, "How could Jesus lower himself and wash the feet of the satanically influenced, the scared, and the selfish?" That question is essential in understanding what washbasin religion is all about.

Jesus lived by the rhythm of the plan of God. He faced the day with an awareness of a scheduled agenda that was set by the Father. He did not operate by an agenda that he set for himself. He lived by one that was established by God the Father. The prophets foretold it. He demonstrated it as early as age twelve. You do remember him telling his mother, Mary, "How is it that you sought me? Know ye not that I must be about my Father's business?" (Luke 2:49).

When Mary came to him concerning the wine that ran out at the wedding feast, his response was that his hour had not yet come. Jesus indicated that he does nothing of himself. He does what the Father reveals. When the Greeks sought for Jesus in Jerusalem, he announced that his time to enter into his glory had come. John notes this in the very first verse of our text. He writes, "Before the Passover celebration, Jesus knew that his hour had come to leave this world and to return to his Father."

Yes, Jesus was sure that the Father had a plan for his life. He could serve in the environment of the satanically influenced, the scared, and the selfish because even it was part of the plan. God allowed such situations and persons to flow Jesus' way because it was within the framework of the plan. Therefore, it was under the control of God. The situation may be uncomfortable, but it's a part of the plan. The Son may not like it, but it's a part of the plan. Likewise, we can serve in the midst of the satanic, the scared, and the selfish when we are sure that the Lord has a plan for our lives.

When we know that the Father has a plan, we also know that God can and will work with whatever circumstance and environment to fulfill the plan. God will take the worst and transform it into that which furthers the plan that God has for us. When we are sure of the plan that God has for us, we are able to celebrate how we're going to end up rather than what we have to endure. The Father has a plan for us to prosper, and to give us a hope and a future. Assurance of the plan of God assures you that God will work all things together for your good and that God will complete whatever he began.

Jesus not only knew of the Father's plan for his life, but he also lived with an understanding of his anointing. In verse three of John 13 we are told, "Jesus knew that the Father had given him authority over everything." Jesus was sure that he had been empowered by God for this time within the plan of God for his life. Jesus faced life and service from the perspective of anointing. You remember him in the temple saying, "The spirit of the Lord is upon me, for he has anointed me to preach the gospel to the poor. He has sent me to proclaim release to the captives, and recovery of sight to the blind, to set the captives free, and to proclaim the acceptable year of the Lord."

Jesus' anointing was recognizable by many who observed that he had authority that was unlike the authority of the Pharisees and scribes. Jesus' authority came from his anointing. There was no circumstance or situation in Christ's life that was allowed by God that was not accompanied with an anointing from God to handle it.

You must be sure of your anointing. When the satanic, the scared, and the selfish surround you, you need the assurance of your anointing. You can't serve under those conditions just because you've got a degree or a stock portfolio. You need more than that. You need the anointing of the Lord. The anointing is the power of God that is given to you by way of the Holy Spirit in order for you to do the will of God. It is God's power that is released in you by way of the Spirit so that you may bring glory and honor unto God. The anointing is the smearing and the rubbing of the personality and power of God upon your life. You must be sure of your anointing. One of the things that the devil could not handle was the anointing that was upon Jesus. That's why you've got to covet the Lord's anointing upon your life. In your anointing is the power to withstand the pull of the demonic and to fulfill the will and way of the Lord for your life. When there are things that are a part of the plan of God that cause discomfort and distress, God will give an anointing to handle them. Somebody knows that had it not been for the anointing of the Lord, you would not have survived. Had it not been for the anointing of God, you would not have survived. Had it not been for the anointing of the Lord, you would have been torn to pieces, ripped to shreds, and fallen apart. What your education could not handle, your anointing did. What your charm could not deal with, your anointing did. What your social connections could not produce, the anointing of God did. The Lord's anointing enabled you to move on, to move ahead, to move onward, and to move upward.

It must be said that the anointing has nothing to do with feeling. The anointing is an objective reality that comes from having the Anointed One in your life. Jesus, who is the Anointed One, lives within the believer by way of the Holy Spirit. The indwelled believer is among the anointed of God. It does not matter how you feel. As a matter of fact, the anointing enables you to serve in spite of your feelings. Jesus did not feel the best with Judas planning to betray him. He wasn't excited about Peter's upcoming denial and the ten's subsequent abandonment. Looking at bread and wine didn't thrill him, knowing that it represented his broken body and shed blood. Notwithstanding the feelings, his anointing empowered him to serve.

Maturity in the anointing of God is demonstrated by operating within your anointing regardless of how you feel. Maturity in the anointing is evidenced by serving when you don't necessarily feel like serving, praying when you don't feel like praying, worshiping when you don't feel like worshiping, and witnessing when you don't necessarily feel like witnessing.

Again John observes in verse three, "Jesus knew that the Father had given him authority over everything and that he had come from God and would return to God." Jesus knew from whence he had come. He was the Word who was with God and who was God. He came from the unscaled heights of glory and through forty-two generations. He also knew where he was going. He was going somewhere. He was going back to the Father. He had a destiny. With a destiny, there is a destination. No one could stop Jesus' destiny or his destination. The demonic forces thought that they could halt Jesus' destiny by arranging for him to be betrayed into the hands of the chief priests, who would then hand him over into the hands of Romans. But Jesus wasn't worried because he knew that his destiny was beyond the chief priests, beyond Herod, beyond the Romans, and beyond the cross. Yes, he would have to face them, but they weren't his destiny nor destination. They were a part of the itinerary, but they weren't his destination. His destination was tied to his destiny. His destiny was to become the author and finisher of our faith, the firstborn from the dead, and the faithful high priest. His destiny was to be highly exalted with a name above every name. His destiny was to become the chief cornerstone. Therefore, his destination was more than his itinerary. It was more than Herod, Pilate, the cross, the tomb, and hell. His destiny was to be raised from the dead, to ascend into heaven, to be seated at the right hand of the throne of God, to prepare a place for believers, to sprinkle the blood in the most holy place, to rapture his church, to vanquish the forces of darkness and to be crowned King of kings and Lord of lords.

Aren't you glad that Jesus served with the towel? You needed him to reach his destination and to fulfill his destiny. You needed a savior, an advocate with the Father, and a high priest who is touched with the feeling of our infirmities. I encourage you to take up the basin and the towel. Let the demonic come.

Let the scared deny you. Let the selfish flee. God's got a plan for your life. God's got an anointing upon your life. There's a destiny and a destination that the Lord has for you. It's yours. It has your name on it. Claim it. Walk in it. Live in it. Celebrate it. Praise God for it. Thank God for it. Thank God that your itinerary is not your destination. Thank God that, while sickness may be on the itinerary, healing is your destination; that while tears may be on the itinerary, joy is your destination; that while storms may be on the itinerary, peace is your destination; that while darkness may be on the itinerary, light is your destination; and that while death may be on the itinerary, it is heaven that is your final destination.

2
A CLOSURE TO THE PAST

RONALD D. BARTON

EXODUS 14:10-13, 20-23, KJV

It is no secret that we stand with our feet firmly planted on the shores of today, never knowing where life will lead nor what progress we will make. We stand at this place with the unknown future before us. In our heart of hearts, we have made up in our minds that we are going to do something to make today better than yesterday. For as much as we look back on the glories of our yesterdays, we must admit that there were some things about yesterday that were not so good. Yesterday there were days of laughter, but we also had days when tears clouded our vision. Yesterday there were heartaches that upset the landscape of our lives. Yesterday there were people whose deeds devastated us and whose words cut our hearts into pieces. Yesterday there were

pains that plummeted us,
predicaments that puzzled us,
mishaps that mesmerized us, and
circumstances that circumvented our happiness.

With all of the things that happened on yesterday, all of us would like to bring closure to many of the events of the past. We do not want the "bad boys" of yesterday hounding us today. We do not want the pains of yesterday to dog us out today. If we would really admit it, what we really desire is closure; for one of the greatest predicaments to face is not being able to close some matter of the past. The worst kind of torment is not being able to resolve some matter of days gone by.

When we look across the fence into the lives of others, we wonder what is wrong with them. We feel like the problem is some matter related to today, but if the truth is revealed, many persons are suffering for a deeper reason. Such people are suffering, not because of today, but because of yesterday. Nobody needs to be beat up by yesterday, for it is only a faint fog behind us. Yesterday is only a memory of what already has taken place.

The fact of the matter is that if you cannot close some things that happened yesterday, you cannot really get on with today. If you cannot close your yesterday, you certainly will not be able to open your tomorrow. You will be like the hapless and hopeless, many of whom are frozen—stranded in time because they have not had closure to the past. They are still dealing with the baggage of history, so they cannot march into their destiny. They are so caught up in what already has happened they cannot begin to see what is about to happen.

It is amazing how God opens revelations through the holy Word, like in this familiar Old Testament story about the children of Israel. I have always been fascinated by their story. The twists and turns of their story make it one that never gets boring, no matter how many times you read it.

In Exodus 14, the Israelites had arrived at the Red Sea. God had opened the way before them. There was, however, a problem. Pharaoh and his troops were in hot pursuit. God's chosen were stranded between dilemma and deliverance. They were stuck between what was and what is to be. In their desperation, many of them begin to cry out, "Were there not enough graves in Egypt that you brought us here to die under the chariot wheels of our former taskmasters?"

God then called Moses into emergency executive session and laid out the plan. Before the people knew it, Moses was climbing up on the rock. Instead of answering their complaints, instead of counteracting their argument, Moses stood and gave a command wrapped up in a promise, "Stand still and see the salvation of the Lord."

In this episode, not only was the promise of the future revealed, but also the never-ending presence of the past. Pharaoh and all of Egypt represented Israel's past, and the land beyond the Red Sea represented their future. If they were going to seize their future, they had to bring closure to their past. In order to move through the open door of what was ahead, they had to close down what was behind. If Pharaoh and Egypt and the past kept coming up, they could never move into the place where God wanted them to be.

In order to get to the new place, the old place has to be dealt with. There has to be closure. Many people are in the same position today that Israel was in then. They have a bright and glorious future before them, but they remain chained by the past. Many a marriage is bogged down because of something in its yesterday. Many churches cannot move into the "new thing" that God promised to do because they are cramped by the struggles of yesterday. In order to move into tomorrow, there has to be a closure on the past.

There are some things that spring out of this story that might help us to gain closure on the past so we can move on. Do not forget the premise of this argument: Pharaoh represents the past; beyond the Red Sea represents the destiny that has been divinely set for Israel. In order to move into their tomorrow, there had to be closure on their past. Let's look at it.

First, it seems like we always encounter our past when we get ready to move toward our future. Here the children of Israel were on their way to the Promised Land. They had been set free. They had marched out of Egypt in a processional of victory. They were inching toward the place where they would live a better life. They would live in a house they did not build. They would eat from trees they did not plant. All of what they needed would be in their new homeland. But just when their future seemed to be within reach, they looked behind them and the past was gaining on them fast.

This always seems to be the case. The past always seems to lie dormant. Like a sleeping lion, the past seems to be at rest. As long as you keep a backward focus, the past keeps on sleeping. As long as you stay put and do not move forward, you never have to encounter the tragedies of yesterday; you never have to encounter the horrors of your history. But just as soon as you make up your mind to move into your tomorrow, you will see your past moving toward you with a vengeance. Things you thought were gone rear their ugly heads once again. You get ready to open the door to your future but the door will not open because you have to keep on dealing with the past.

Even the enemy knows that if you keep dealing with yesterday long enough, you will become afraid to move into the future. The children of Israel had started to believe that the pharaoh of their past was no more than a faint notation on the pages of their history—merely a footnote to their years of slavery and struggle. But what better way to keep them from moving forward? Just let them keep on dealing with the issues of their past! It would take their nerve away, their will away, their trust away, their optimism away, and ultimately it would take their destiny away.

Some of you are afraid of the future because matters of the past keep coming at you, but God has opened up the way so that you can move to the divinely designed place. So when you have to encounter the past, do not let it distract you because if God has opened the way, it has been done so that you might move into your future.

The second thing that seemed a little strange—if you read the text closely—is that it seemed like the past and the future were on the same path. They were on their way, crossing the Red Sea. God swung open before them a path to victory. With a blast of God's nostrils and the might of divine will, the Red Sea, which was a barrier to hem them in, became a highway to bring them out. But as they got to the other side, they looked back, and on the same path behind them they saw the past gaining on them. Why did it seem like God would allow the victory of their tomorrow and the agents of their yesterday to be on the same path?

The Holy Spirit helped me with that. The reason why you often can look back down the same path and see the past and the future is that a glance at what was should motivate you to move forward into what can be. When you look over your shoulder and see what you have been through, that gives you a reason to move ahead. When you look back and see the negative and nasty things that you had to deal with yesterday, that glimpse makes you hurry toward tomorrow. You hurry because you do not want to relive that pain; you do not want to relive that tragedy. So when you see your past behind you, then you ought to move with determination into the place that God has set before you.

The final point to the story is that God will bring closure to your past. God will never allow your past to catch up with your progress. The Lord has a way of bringing closure to your past. Look at Israel. Pharaoh's army was gaining on them. They had reached the other side but the army was still coming. Their hopes were vanishing. The victory seemed to be slipping through their hands. The gap between them seemed to be closing. The past was gaining on them, but God is an excellent God. The Lord will never allow your used-to-be's to gain victory over your about-to-be's.

*Their used-to-be's wanted to intimidate them, but their
about-to-be's encouraged them.*

*Their used-to-be's wanted to scare them, but their
about-to-be's gave them strength.*

*Their used-to-be's wanted to bring up their pain and
predicament, but their about-to-be's wanted them
to see their deliverance.*

*Their used-to-be's wanted them to remember their past,
but their about-to-be's wanted to show them their future.*

Pharaoh did not have enough sense to realize that if God opened up the Red Sea for Israel, God also could close it up once the people had reached safety. God shut down the past. God closed the matter by closing the Red Sea. Before bondage could reclaim Israel, the Lord closed the Red Sea and Pharaoh's army drowned.

What's this? Pharaoh did not drown with them. Why was he kept alive? Pharaoh was the ruler, the potentate, and the authority. Why was he kept alive? God used Pharaoh to teach us something. God does not always eliminate every part of our past, but God does strip the power from our past so that it can no longer have power over us. The symbol of the past can be there, but the power of the past will be gone. Regardless of the past,

I'm pressing on the upward way,
New heights I'm gaining everyday.
Still praying as I'm onward bound,
"Lord plant my feet on higher ground."[1]

God be praised that he can bring closure to the past!

NOTE

1. "Higher Ground," lyrics by Johnson Oatman Jr. Public domain.

3

WHEN GOOD PEOPLE DO BAD THINGS

CHARLES E. BOOTH

GENESIS 16:1-6, NIV

Several years ago, Harold S. Kushner wrote an acclaimed national bestseller entitled *When Bad Things Happen to Good People.*[1] Rabbi Kushner wrote this book out of the crucible of his personal pain. Following the birth of their daughter, Kushner and his wife were informed that their three-year-old son, Aaron, was dying from a disease called *progeria*, for which there was no cure. This awesome affliction meant that the boy would age rapidly. Aaron would never grow beyond three feet in height, would have no hair on his head or body, would look like a little old man while still a child, and would in all probability die in his early teens.

The pediatrician's prognosis had pinpoint accuracy, for Aaron died at the age of fourteen. This heart-wrenching experience forced Rabbi Kushner to raise the ancient and forever agonizing question, "Why do the righteous suffer?" Or we must ponder, in the chosen language of this Jewish rabbi, "When bad things happen to good people!" This is the question of theodicy with which we all wrestle; and as a result of this wrestling match, there is a question that will forever haunt us: "If God is good, then why is there the presence, power, and persistence of evil?"

I raise this as a point of departure because I am confident that many of you thought I had mislabeled the subject of this message. Not so at all. While the question of theodicy is a vital question, it is not the issue with which I wrestle in this message. It is my desire to deal with another issue equally as close to home, but one that Christians do not like to face. Whether we admit it or not, the human experience is cluttered with the reality that *good* people do *bad* things. Sarai, who later becomes Sarah, is the subject of this message. She is married to Abram, who later becomes Abraham. At the time of this text, Sarai is an old woman approaching her eighties. She is barren and has been denied the opportunity to bear children. Sarai loves her husband, Abram, and would delight in nothing more than to give him a child. Since Sarai is beyond childbearing age, she comes to what she considers to be a thoughtful decision. She will allow her husband, who very much exceeds the years of an octogenarian, to lie with Hagar, her Egyptian maidservant, as his wife. She hopes that Hagar, as surrogate, might produce a child, long desired by the aged couple. Sarai considers this course of action to be the solution to her problem. There is a note of humor at this point in the story because Abram gives no indication that he is at variance with his wife's suggestion. If I were to contemporize this moment in the text, I can imagine Abram securing a prescription for Viagra from his urologist and presenting himself to Hagar with the exuberant declaration, "Let the good times roll!"

It is not long before Hagar acknowledges her pregnancy and begins to "strut her stuff" before Sarai, for the text says in verse 4: "When she knew she was pregnant, she began to despise her mistress." While Sarai has every reason to be upset, she wrongly blames Abram for what has occurred. As a result, verse 6 says, "Then Sarai mistreated Hagar." Nowhere in the record are we told that Sarai is a bad person. In fact, her very name means "princess." She had married Abram long ago in Ur of the Chaldees and followed him to Canaan without debate. While she loved her husband and her God, Sarai could not tolerate the taunting and teasing of this black servant girl from Egypt whose womb now bore the growing fetus whose paternity is Abram's.

Thus, Sarai mistreats Hagar. Sarai is a good person, but she now begins doing bad things. All of us can identify with Sarai because we learned early in life that one does not have to be a bad person to do a bad thing. I am convinced that our penal institutions are filled with good people who are simply guilty of having done something bad. Why did Sarai mistreat Hagar? Why do good people do bad things?

Sarai mistreats Hagar, in the first instance, because of embarrassment and humiliation. Hagar's behavior prompted Sarai to do what many of us do when hurt and impugned—strike back. She was putting into practice the Old Testament axiom of an "eye for an eye and a tooth for a tooth." It was as if Sarai was saying, "You hurt me, so I'll hurt you! You embarrass me, so I'll embarrass you! You humiliate me, so I'll humiliate you!" No one delights in being the target of embarrassment and humiliation. All of us delight in being the center of attention when we are being positively applauded and praised. However, it is a horse of another color when we become public spectacles.

It cannot be denied that Hagar is the genesis of the problem because it is she who parades her pregnancy in a public forum before the glaring infertility of Sarai. But one must know that at the root of Sarai's embarrassment and humiliation is an even greater haunting. Sarai is haunted by the consequences of her own decision. Hagar was not pregnant because of Abram's indiscretion. He did not go out and simply impregnate another woman. Hagar was not some "loose" woman who just threw herself at another woman's husband. Honesty would have to compel Sarai to admit that this situation was her own creation! At first, it seemed like a good idea. On the surface, Sarai thought this plan to be the ideal remedy to her problem of infertility. Eastern occidental women did it all the time. When a woman could not bear her husband a child, it was not uncommon for the wife to seek a surrogate. This was an ancient and acceptable practice of that day and time. To Sarai, it all seemed so logical, reasonable, and rational. However, Sarai never stopped to think about how the surrogate mother would flaunt her pregnancy, nor did she take into account her own feelings and emotions. Sometimes we mistreat others because we cannot deal with the consequences of our own bad decisions. We victimize others when our own plans fail!

One of Newton's great laws is that every action has an equal and opposite reaction, and from a spiritual perspective, every decision has a consequence. All of us are guilty of having made some bad decisions, and often, we pay sorely for such decisions. This is why we must be thoughtful and prayerful about the decisions we make. Paul is right when he declares that whatsoever a person sows, that shall the person also reap (Galatians 6:7). We always are encountering people who never take into consideration the consequences of their decisions. The person who elects to use illegal drugs seldom takes into consideration the consequences of such activity to the body and mind. Persons who engage in promiscuous sexual activity do not always consider the threat of sexually transmitted diseases and the HIV/AIDS epidemic.

One of the great tragedies of our time is that children often are abused physically, emotionally, and psychologically because of parents who have not been able to deal with the consequences of bad decisions. Parents unequally yoked! Parents unable to deal with a frustration or guilt that goes back many years! Parents existing in a loveless marriage! Parents forced to marry because of an unplanned pregnancy! Parents who live with unrealized ambition never secured a college education because they had to "drop out" in order to provide for the family. Good people do bad things because we sometimes do not realize just how impaling our decisions can be.

Secondly, Sarai mistreats Hagar because her status is potentially threatened. Being unable to produce a child in the ancient world of Abram and Sarai might have meant more than embarrassment and humiliation. In many instances, it was considered a disgrace. The barren wife could be reduced to the status of a slave if she did not produce a male heir for her husband. One must not forget what verse 3 says: "Sarai, his wife, took her

Egyptian maidservant Hagar and gave her to her husband to be his wife."

Hagar is not simply a surrogate or substitute mother. Hagar becomes Abram's other wife in a permissible, polygamous arrangement. Sarai has to protect her own self-interest. One must remember that Hagar is not a slave, but a maidservant. Abram and Sarai are not in Canaan. They are in Egyptian territory, which is North Africa. It is very unlikely that Egyptians would allow these nomadic, traveling Jews to enslave one of their own. The slaves owned by the Egyptians at this point in history are Asiatic. Thus, in Hagar, Abram and Sarai were able to acquire a beautiful, black servant girl who is not a slave.

One can plainly see now why Hagar was "strutting her stuff." She is really in an ambiguous situation. On the one hand, Hagar is the servant of Sarai. But now she is also the wife of Abram. With the birth of a male child, Hagar knows that she can replace Sarai, not only in Abram's affections, but also in the hierarchy of the polygamous arrangement. Sarai does not want to be disgraced or reduced to a lesser status because of this black girl who is about to produce Abram's male heir. Sarai is threatened; not only is Sarai's status threatened, but her security as well. If Sarai is reduced to a slave and is no longer Abram's wife, then she must vacate the master bedroom, give up the credit cards, relinquish the Mercedes Benz, cancel all hair and nail appointments, and forget about her "first lady" status. Sarai cannot handle the possibility of such losses. Thus, she mistreats Hagar.

Sounds familiar, does it not? People have been known to do bad things in order to maintain their status and security. This is why racism is so deeply entangled in our nation. Racism is predicated on the belief that one race is superior to another, or even to all others. The current assault on affirmative action is the dominant culture's way of asserting that minorities have enough. It is all right for a few African Americans to get good jobs and promotions, but not too many. We of the African American community must not hesitate to declare that a few years of affirmative action cannot atone for 244 years of free slave labor and 381 years of ceaseless racism in America. Whenever the status and security of the majority culture are threatened, we can expect mistreatment.

During the summer of 1998, Supreme Court Justice Clarence Thomas was invited to address the annual meeting of the National Bar Association. There was some debate as to whether or not Justice Thomas should speak before this African American assembly of attorneys given his position on affirmative action. Justice Thomas defended his anti-affirmative action position and went on to say that he allows no one to set his agenda for him. This could not possibly be true, for it appears that Justice Thomas has allowed the conservative political might of the dominant culture to very much set his agenda.

The Honorable Judge A. Leon Higginbotham was asked by Brit Hume, political analyst for the Fox television network, to comment on Justice Thomas's speech. Mr. Hume commented that Justice Thomas should be applauded for having come so far in the light of his Pin Point, Georgia, beginnings. It was at this juncture that Judge Higginbotham reminded Mr. Hume that such a rise from poverty was not uncommon for African Americans. He went on to point out that most successful African Americans emerged from poor beginnings. The judge was seeking to point out that Clarence Thomas is only one of thousands of blacks who emerged out of poverty, was given an opportunity, and succeeded. The problem is that, unlike other African Americans, Clarence Thomas seems to have forgotten his roots and slammed shut the very door that got him into the Yale University Law School. The point is clear; Justice Thomas has played into the hands of the enemy! It is as if the dominant culture is saying, "We'll let you in, but you have to shut the door!" It is all about status and security.

One must never become threatened and insecure when another person is allowed to achieve and succeed. We are all God's children! I need not mistreat you in order to succeed in my quest.

If Booker T. Washington had had Clarence Thomas's attitude, we would not have Tuskegee University!

If W.E.B. Du Bois had had Clarence Thomas's attitude, we would not have *The Souls of Black Folk!*

If Adam Clayton Powell Jr. had had Clarence Thomas's attitude, we would not have National Direct Student Loans and the minimum wage!

If Montgomery, Birmingham, and "I Have a Dream!" had had Clarence Thomas's attitude . . .

The song we sing does not proclaim, "If I can hurt, hamper or hinder somebody!" It says, "If I can help somebody!"

Finally, Sarai mistreated Hagar because of human nature; regardless of how good we think we are, we are never good enough. There is something in all of us that makes us go awry at times! All of us have crooked ways that need to be made straight and rough plains that need to be smooth. We are "naughty by nature!" Education, economics, and pedigree are never enough. Hagar was a tease! Sarai mistreated Hagar! Abram lied! Jacob was deceptive! Moses was a murderer! Samson was sexually weak! David committed adultery! Solomon unfairly and unduly taxed his own people! James and John were egotists! Peter was impetuous! Paul persecuted the church! It is an undeniable fact of history that good people do bad things! But thanks be to God, this is not our eternal plight and destiny! There is One who is good totally and completely! There is One who is lovely altogether! There is One who is wonderful, counselor, mighty God, and Prince of Peace! He is Jesus, the Christ! It is he who can do for us what we can never do for ourselves! He is the only One who can save us from our sins and from ourselves! Good people do bad things, but good people can be forgiven and begin again!

NOTE

1. Harold S. Kushner, *When Bad Things Happen to Good People* (New York: William Morrow & Company, 1982).

4
LET'S CELEBRATE!
JOHN R. BRYANT
LUKE 15:22-24, TLB

The renowned poet Lucille Clifton has a captivating line in one of her poems that extends a marvelous invitation. Listen as she invites,

Come celebrate with me
for every day something has tried to kill me
and has failed.

This is an invitation that all of us can extend. This is an invitation that the young, old, poor, rich, male, female, learned, and unlearned can extend. Come celebrate, come rejoice, come and party with me, "for every day something has tried to kill me / and has failed."

All that was designed against us has failed. There are over a million diseases capable of destroying human life—blood disorders, heart conditions, tumors, and so forth. All of them are capable of taking our lives, yet we continue to survive. The air is polluted, the water is polluted, and much of our food is contaminated. We breathe this polluted air in and out of our lungs. We drink this polluted water. We eat this contaminated food, and yet we survive. Oh yes, we can extend the invitation, "Come celebrate with me, for every day something has tried to kill me / and has failed."

We also ought to celebrate because we have survived

ourselves. Each one of us has survived our own personal mistakes—the bad choices, the poor decisions, the indiscretions, and the personal weaknesses. So much of the trouble we have gotten into has been self-inflicted. We have said something, thought something, or done something we should not have. We have lied to ourselves. We have spent too much time covering up our flaws, attempting to hide them from ourselves. Each one of us has talked ourselves into doing things that could have destroyed us.

The story is told of a man who goes to another friend's house for a Saturday morning visit. When the friend opens the door, he sees that there are fresh wounds on the visiting man's face. When the friend inquires about the wounds, the man confesses that he drank too much the night before. While intoxicated, the phone rang, and he reached for what he thought was the phone to hold it to his ear. But instead he had picked up a hot iron and burned his ear with it! The friend said how sorry he was that it had happened; but then he inquired, "Well, that explains how one side was burned, but what happened to the other side?"

"Well," the man answered, "the fool called me back."

So many of us have been burned more than once by something we said we would not repeat. We have brought situations into our lives that caused us severe problems. Yet after working our way out of the particular problem, we found ourselves returning to the very source of the problem. But in spite of all our bad choices, we have survived. So let's celebrate! For we have overcome our self-inflicted wounds.

The devil wanted you dead. I can say to you what Jesus said to Peter, "The devil wants to sift you like wheat." The devil wanted to kill you with drugs, alcohol, food, depression, a broken heart, and stress. The devil tried to drive you insane, tried kill you in that automobile accident, tried to convince you that you were a loser and that life itself was not worth living. Satan sent his demon spirits to stalk you on that job, in that marriage, and even tried to turn your own children against you, but you survived. You came through all of it. Come on, let's celebrate!

For every day, something has tried to destroy you, and failed.

But for those still struggling for this level of victorious living, I want to deposit in your spirit a major key. Every believer must recognize those things that deserve to be celebrated—and do not let anything in you or outside of you block your celebration. The act of celebration is extremely positive. When you celebrate, it suggests more than joy. It also suggests victory. That which ought be celebrated is proof that God has been acting on your behalf. It is evidence that God has been working for your victory. Those who do not know that they are victorious will adopt the attitude of a loser.

A loser is an easy receptacle for the devil's deposit of all that is negative. But if you know that in Christ Jesus you are more than a conqueror, you will overcome the negative obstacles of life and put the devil under your feet. Those who are committed to victorious living do not wallow in the negatives of the past. They stand on their tiptoes, looking expectantly for the next blessing. Their faith tells them that the God in whom they believe has something in store that will be worth celebrating.

The text for this message teaches the value of celebration. William Barclay writes that this narrative is misnamed. It is traditionally referred to as the "Story of the Prodigal Son," but Barclay writes that it ought to be known as the "Story of the Loving Father." I would go a step farther and call it the "Story of the Victorious Father." For the father of the prodigal son demonstrates how, in spite of life's reversals, one can still live victoriously.

Dr. Luke tells us, in the fifteenth chapter of his Gospel, of a father who had two sons. The younger son demanded that the father divide his wealth and give him his share. In other words, he was demanding his inheritance while his father was still alive. The father did not fight with his younger son; instead, he granted his younger son's request. This in itself would have been enough to make many men very bitter; but the story does not indicate that the father assumed this posture. The son was, at the very least, inconsiderate; however, the father was wise enough to know that sometimes life itself is the best teacher.

The Bible informs us that the boy went to a far country with his new wealth. It did not take him long to lose all of his father's hard-earned money. He fell on "hard times," and found himself working with pigs. He was hungry, he was broke, and he was far from home. He then came to himself. He decided to return to his father's house and ask for a second chance. The beautiful thing about the Christian faith is that it allows the believer another, and another, and another chance. The prodigal son did not know whether the father would receive him, but he did know that even his father's servants were living better than he was living.

The son knew his father had something he needed. The father had provisions, and the son needed them. The father had love, and he needed to be loved. The father was a source of hope, and the son needed hope in his life. The father, in Luke's narrative, had the right attitude for a victorious life. Even though the son was inconsiderate in his departure, the father did not allow the son's actions to make him a bitter man. The father, I believe, had a level of hope that caused him to await his son's return.

The Bible said the father saw his son coming from a distance. I like to imagine the father standing on the front porch waiting for the son's return. Those who intend to live a victorious life must stand on the front porch of their existence looking for something to celebrate. When the father saw his son coming, he did not see a loser or a failure. He saw the Lord's answer to his prayers. He saw his victory. The father ran to his son, kissed him, and called for a great celebration.

When the older brother returned home and saw that everyone was in a mood of celebration, he became upset. The elder son could not celebrate because he could not see what his father could see. If you cannot see your blessings, you cannot celebrate. The elder brother could not see that God was at work. He did not see that the father's love for him was constant. He could not see what God had delivered his brother from. The father had to help his older son to see.

This is the role of the church. The church must help people to see the hand of the Lord in their lives. The ministry of the Word must encourage people to look more carefully until they see that in their lives there are reasons to celebrate. The father had to help his son see that they had to celebrate, for the brother who was lost had been found. The elder son also needed to be reminded that he had been living all along in his father's loving provision for him.

Children of God, let's celebrate! Open your eyes and look at all that the Lord has done for us. Let's celebrate the blessings that are ours in the present moment. Let's celebrate the lordship of Jesus Christ in our lives. Realize that because of His lordship, we have future blessings in store. Let's celebrate the fact that "every day with Jesus is sweeter than the day before."

Come on, I know you have some problems, but thank God you have more than problems. You have a God who has been good to you. So stop frowning and put a smile on your face. Get your shouting shoes out, and let the party begin!

5

WHY NOT ME?

WILLIAM H. CURTIS

ACTS 1:21-26, KJV

After the ascension of Jesus, the disciples overcame the temptation to live stuck gazing at the glory that transported the Savior from time into eternity. Those who witnessed the resurrected Lord decided it was time to get back to everyday life and get busy working for the kingdom.

First on their agenda was filling the void left in the apostolic group when Judas killed himself for betraying the Lord to his enemies. Judas' death created an opening, and God's desire was that the apostolic group would number twelve. This number symbolized the Old Testament tribes of Israel. John would later reveal in the Book of Revelation that heaven has twelve special positions awaiting those who worked in the apostolic band (Revelation 22:14).

There was work to be done, and before the coming of the Holy Spirit, this infant gathering, this spiritual remnant, this small band of believers that was the church, had to position herself in the order of God to prepare for what God was going to bring next.

To facilitate the process, Peter stood and took principal leadership and authority. He suggested that they ought to fill the void immediately. Everybody agreed, and in verse 21, Peter laid out the criteria for apostolic inclusion.

First, he said, the person has to be somebody who has been with us from the beginning until Jesus was taken up from us. Why? Because our witness must include the resurrection, and that leads us to the second criterion.

We need folks who can tell people more than just "Jesus lived and he died." That will not give hope to people. What will give hope to people is an eyewitness account to the fact that he lived, he died, and he was resurrected from the grave.

Notice that this is what became an issue when, years later, Paul claimed apostleship, because he was far removed from being an authentic and actual witness to the resurrected Lord. Paul lay claim to apostleship because what the disciples saw in the physical, he had seen in the spiritual while he was on the road to Damascus. He used the new theological understanding to demand that they give him the right hand of fellowship as an apostle to the Gentiles.

When Peter had finished speaking to his fellow believers, the Bible reveals that two men who fit the criteria were identified: Joseph (called Barsabas), and Matthias. The people went through a process, and when they finished Matthias was chosen to become part of the Twelve who would lead the kingdom project to evangelize the world.

When Matthias was chosen, you can see with your spiritual eyes that everybody was celebrating. I admit that when I read it, I, too, said "Good! Now they can get on with the work of ministry and carry on the proclamation of the gospel." But my spirit would not let me rest there. I kept thinking, not about the one chosen, but the one who was not chosen. What about Joseph, the man God did not choose? How do you live with the fact that you are the one not chosen?

What do you say to a person who was one of only two candidates? Everybody is celebrating with the one chosen, while the unchosen asks, "But what about me?"

I will be honest: I know more Josephs than Matthiases. The church is full of Josephs. They are in our families. They love the Lord, but things just have not worked out for them like they have for you or others they know.

Or maybe you are Joseph and you are saying "Amen" right now because you are wondering why other Christians can be less faithful and yet more blessed, while here you are trying to be more faithful. You are catching it from every corner, and you are tired of living as the one not selected. And the church—if it is to be a church—cannot just celebrate with Matthias. We also must minister to and embrace Joseph.

Joseph must feel comfortable that it is all right to be the one not chosen, not get the job, not make the engagement work, not have doors open, not make the marriage last, or not make decisions that work.

Joseph could have asked, "Isn't it my turn yet? Like everyone else, I have given my time, my talent, and my tenure. I have been focused, faithful, and following. When is it my turn to get some of what I want, to have things flow my way, to make things successful for me? When is it my turn to get a day up front rather than from the back? When is it my turn to be selected first or considered valuable? When is it my turn?"

My friends, we need to minister to Joseph because at some point we are all Joseph—not picked, not selected, not included, without things going our way. What makes this kind of rejection so bad is that God did it. The one not chosen must acknowledge the fact that "God didn't pick me." The lesson is this—we must help people to understand that being the one not chosen does not mean "I am a failure," or a reject.

God wants me to celebrate me, not my selection, because there are a whole lot of folks selected who are not ready for what they have been selected to do.

Both men were presented because they were ready. Joseph would not have been considered had he not been ready to be chosen. He had what it took to work among the Twelve. He was able to handle the job. He could have been good at it, so not being selected did not mean he was not ready.

There are some things that I will not be selected for, but that I am ready for. Why does this happen? It happens because some things are affected by human error, and some things are affected by unclear and cloudy discernment, and some things God reserves the right to delay even though you are ready.

Joseph could leave saying, "I didn't get that position, but I was ready for it." That is what God wants each of us to develop in our spirits. My not getting something does not mean I was not ready for it. I do not celebrate the rejection, but the readiness.

I didn't get the job, but I was ready for it.

I didn't get the promotion, but I was ready for it.

I didn't get selected, but I was able and ready for it.

That is the key in the kingdom—not selection, but readiness. Don't ever get drunk on the culture's need to measure success by selection. That is too results oriented. Your readiness is a sign that you have navigated your life in a way that would have caused others to give up, and yet you are still standing. When others were eliminated, you were still holding on. Selection is not always a sign of success, but readiness is.

PROVIDENCE CAN NEVER BE MANIPULATED BY HUMAN DESIRE

The providence of God is not subject to our desires and wishes. God does not blindly obey us. God expects us to, in faith, be obedient. God is free to choose whom God wants, when God wants. That is a hard fact for the human mind and spirit to process because that means God can choose not to choose me, and I must trust that. I must remember that in spite of the fact that God may not choose me, God still loves me and takes care of me. How do I do that?

We do this by trusting the integrity of the process. Those gathered in Jerusalem prayed that God would search their hearts. Joseph could find encouragement in that because after they prayed, the believers were still confused about which of the men should be included and which one should not, so they then cast lots.

Now this is interesting because Acts 1:26 is the only place in the New Testament where you read about the Lord's people casting lots to discern God's will. In this instance, according to practice, they got two sticks and inscribed Matthias's name on one stick, and Joseph's name on the other. They then placed the two sticks in a garment called a lap. Then someone shook the garment until one of the sticks fell out. They trusted that God would let only the name of the person chosen to fall out. So when Matthias's name fell out, Joseph didn't complain, he didn't argue, and he didn't start confusion. He accepted the Lord's will and lived on. He understood providence.

If there is a hard lesson that the church must teach, it is this: You can pray, pay your tithes, and worship God in spirit and in truth, yet there still will be times when God will choose to do what you do not want God to do. Sometimes God will not choose you, or your desires and wishes, to accomplish divine will.

Remember, Joseph already was doing what every other disciple was doing. He fit the criteria that Peter had laid out. Joseph was with Jesus from the beginning. He had seen Christ in resurrected splendor. He had everything necessary to be called an apostle, but what he did not get was the title.

I am excited about this because I think that if I were there, and Joseph, Barsabas, or Justus—whichever name he might have used to introduce himself—came into my office and started complaining, I would have listened to him talk about how qualified he was: "How dare they overlook me! Why did God not think I could handle the work?"

Then I would have counseled him this way: "Joseph, you are right. You have been working and witnessing just like the rest of the brothers. You have seen just what they saw and you know just what they know. So I, too, wondered why God would not choose you to be an apostle. And the Lord revealed this: Some folks need to be chosen because they need titles in order to do the work. But God knew that even if you were not selected to wear the title, you would still do the work."

Isn't it true that so many in the church need titles to be good Christians? Don't ever get caught up in thinking that you need to have a title in the church.

You don't need to be called a missionary in order to
    witness and show hospitality to strangers.
You don't have to be a trustee to care for the facility.
You don't need to be a choir member to sing a new song.
You don't need to be a preacher to tell somebody about
    how good the Lord is, and that God can save and
    deliver.
You don't have to be an usher to welcome somebody
    into the house of God.
You don't have to be in charge in order to take charge
    and bind on earth what shall be bound in heaven.
I don't have to be the one to gain all the glory,
I don't have to be the one to tell the story,
Not for title or status.
All that I ask is that you use me. Please, Lord, use me.

6

THE PREACHER'S
PREDICAMENT

H. BEECHER HICKS JR.

EPHESIANS 6:18-20, KJV

There is a common predicament among preachers that I suspect is a consequence of the nature of the prophetic office we hold. From the moment one hears and heeds the summons to be engaged in this perilous occupation we call preaching, there is a perplexing, peculiar pain that is surely attendant to that summons. It is a pain that resides somewhere between the agony and ecstasy of preaching's claim and call. So peculiar is this pain, so confining is this condition, that one is hard pressed to define it. But Abraham knew his predicament the moment God sent him in search of a land that no one else could locate.

Moses became acquainted with this pain the moment God sent him to Egypt. God sent him out with a stick and a stutter. Moses was summoned to lead a nation with a stick and to stutter out a sermon that seemed to make no sense.

Habakkuk was introduced to this pain predicament the moment he realized that in order to be heard he would be required to take up residence in the city tower and then write the vision so a man running could read it.

If the truth were told, you and I are acquainted with this pain because, very often, what God requires of us, and what God expects of us, are separated from what we believe we are realistically able to achieve. The truth is that, very often, what God wants and what God demands ignores the church politics around us, ignores the limitations of our financial resources, requires that we think in "God-sized" terms while we work with "midget-sized" minds, and literally expects us to produce miracles where, heretofore, miracles were never found.

What God wants, what God requires, and what God demands unsettles the psyche; it disturbs sleep, it agitates the spirit, it causes unrest among those who are called to preach, and it breeds discontent among the people we are commissioned to lead and to whom we are instructed to preach. For these reasons, I am convinced that there is a predicament, common among preachers, that comes as a consequence of the nature of the prophetic office we hold.

On the other hand, just as there is a predicament common among preachers, there is also a resistance common among those who fill the pews where we preach. It is a resistance that both mitigates and militates against the task we are summoned to achieve.

Not many preachers come to the pulpit declaring, "Thus saith the Lord . . ." anymore, primarily because, in this age, no one would believe that a mortal being can speak for an immortal God. At the very moment in human history when God's Word desperately needs to be heard, we are faced with an issue of credibility and believability. This is a predicament.

But God keeps on calling preachers to preach. In fact, there are so many preachers claiming to have been called to preach that nobody knows for certain who is a preacher and who is not. That is a predicament.

The very nature of the calling to which we have been summoned empowers us to speak the Word of God to the people of God on behalf of God. But in this day of sophisticated communication, in order to be relevant, in order to be connected, it looks like God needs to speak by way of the Internet; God needs to send e-mail, or God needs a Web site. Nobody wants to believe that, of all the ways in which God could communicate, that God would choose such frail, flawed vessels. These men and women who are not always fleet of mind or agile of tongue, these men and women whose feet are made of clay, whose steps are prone to wander, and whose lives are stained with the indelible ink of sin—that God would take these kinds of people, that God would take us, and entrust us, and empower us, with a divine Word is more than the mind can imagine. That is a predicament. That is why—in case I have not told you—I am convinced that there is a predicament, common among preachers, that comes as a consequence of the nature of the prophetic office we hold.

This predicament of which I speak is common not only to those of us who preach, but was common as well to an itinerant preacher from Tarsus whom we know as Paul. Paul . . . the apostle Paul . . . the Right Reverend Dr. Paul . . . more than any other, stood in the preacher's predicament:

> Called, and yet at the same time, reviled for his calling.
> Tormented by an inescapable "urge" to preach and at the same time tormented by those who did not wish to hear his preaching.
> Certain that God had laid the divine hand on him but also certain that enemies and foes had come upon him to eat up his flesh.
> Certain that God had called him to preach, but at the same time, certain that, as he said, "When I would do good, evil is present with me" (Romans 7:21).
> Confident that he had been sent to liberate others; yet at the same time, he himself was imprisoned.

Imprisoned. That is the word I am seeking. Paul describes his predicament and describes himself as a prisoner. To hear Paul tell it, everybody else calls him a preacher; but in fact, says Paul, "I am a prisoner." The reason why Paul knows that he is a prisoner is because of his chains. Don't you find it strange that when Paul referred to himself, he referred to himself as a prisoner in chains, a prisoner in bonds? Listen to his language:

"I Paul, the prisoner of Jesus Christ for you Gentiles..."
    (Ephesians 3:1).
"I therefore, the prisoner of the Lord, beseech you that ye
    walk worthy of the vocation wherewith ye are called"
    (Ephesians 4:1).
"Be not thou therefore ashamed of the testimony of our
    Lord, nor of me his prisoner..." (2 Timothy 1:8).

Then, here in these last lines of his writings to the church at
Ephesus, Paul reaches for eloquent definition and speaks of him-
self as an "ambassador in bonds" (Ephesians 6:20). Listen to what
Paul says.

When I think of myself, I am a preacher, but I am also a
prisoner. When I think of myself, I am a courier, but I am also
a convict. I have a gospel that sets others free but when I look
at myself, I am looking at my chains. That is why you need
to pray for me because, among other things, I am an ambassador
in bonds.

I have serious concerns for those who come to the engagement of ministry with no sense of "fear and trembling." I am concerned about a breed of persons who perceive ministry and come
to the ministry, not because of a divine summons, but because of
a vocational choice. I rise to tell you that this preaching business
is about chains. The one who claims to have been "called" does
not know it, but he or she is on the way to chains. The robes we
wear are really nothing more than parish garb. These suits we
wear really ought to have stripes because we are really in con-
victs' clothing. Everywhere I go, I tend to attract attention; not
because of who I am, but because of my chains.

I am not here by choice; I am here because of a warrant that
has arrested me, confined me, altered my perspective, and
rearranged my life. My position here is about chains. My
predicament is such that, when you see me, you must understand
that what I look like externally is not what I am internally—I am
an ambassador in bonds.

Let me assure you that there is no diplomatic immunity from

the bond predicament. If you are a preacher worthy of the name, you have some bond time coming. If it is your assignment to "cry aloud and spare not" (Isaiah 58:1), if it is your appointed duty to preach the unsearchable riches of our Christ, then it will not be very long before you become acquainted with your chains.

I have come here confined in my bonds, dressed in these chains. Here I am, insulted by my chains, and I want to know why I must wear these chains. There is something strange about the garb I am wearing. This is not exactly the ecclesiastical attire I was looking for.

I have been given to understand that I am an ambassador. That means I have status and stature. That means I have rank and title. My credentials authorize my entrance into places of social and political power. Evidently, somebody doesn't know who I am! I have standing with the King. I am here to speak the words that the King has put in my mouth. When folk see me coming, they know that I bear the imprimatur of the Monarch. But, I am still in these chains.

There must be some cause for the predicament I am in. If, by surface examination, I open up this Pauline text in what Markus Barth refers to as "Paul's puzzling epistle," it becomes clear that the source of my confinement is in the nature of the institution with which I am involved. In other words, the church itself is part of and parcel to my predicament.

Paul says that the source of my predicament is in the church. The thing that frustrates me is not what goes on in city hall, but what goes on in the church. Those who have the most severe questions about the leadership of the church and the vision for the church are not outside the church, but inside! I do not have a problem with the winos or the drug addicts on the corner; the problem I have is with the saved and the sanctified on the front pew on the right-hand side.

I didn't say it; Paul said it: "We wrestle not against flesh and blood, but against principalities, against powers, against the rulers of the darkness of this world, against spiritual wickedness in high places" (Ephesians 6:12).

The thing that concerns me is "spiritual wickedness," that
wickedness that wears church clothes.
That wickedness that wears badges and choir robes.
That wickedness that knows how to speak church talk,
but will curse you out in the parking lot.
That wickedness that knows how to speak in tongues and
dance a holy dance, but won't say "Good morning" to
the person sitting on the same pew.
That wickedness that knows how to carry a Bible, but will
not read it; knows how to lift up "Holy Hands," but
will not lend a helping hand.
The problem we face is not in the world, it is in the church.
The reason I am in these chains is not because of what somebody
did "out there," but because of what somebody did in here. That
is a predicament.

I am searching still for the reason for these chains. It could be
that the reason for my chains is that . . .

AUTHENTIC PREACHING IS ALWAYS
A PRODUCT OF PAIN

The other day, while walking through National Airport in
Washington, D.C., I saw a young man, neatly dressed and handsome in appearance. There was nothing exceptionally remark-
able about him except he could hardly walk because of his
chains. A guard was standing by, no doubt delivering him from
one jail cell to another. Yet, when taking more than a casual
glance, I could see the hurt in his eyes, the sadness in his soul,
and the humiliation in the stoop of his shoulders.

I am not sure how this works, but somehow it is out of my pain
that my preaching is produced. That preaching is authentic
when it comes. . . .

FROM PAIN TO PAIN

I must never forget while in the process of my preaching that
someone before me is in pain. While I preach from my pulpit,
there is someone with a broken spirit in my pew.

I must never forget that while I am writing out the order of worship, somebody is coming through the door whose life is not orderly and could care less about what you print in your bulletin.

Because my pews are "filled with pain," I must be sensitive to the pain in me that enables me to speak to the pain in them.

It is out of the experiences in my life that bring water to my eyes that I am able to minister to those whose eyes are wet with fresh tears.

When I stand under the scrutiny of my own sin, I am able to understand the necessity for grace.

When I am able to acknowledge my own weakness and my own frailty, I am able to point those who sit before me to a rock that is higher than I.

When I am able to see for myself that I have been wounded and beaten, when I am able to see beyond my turned-around collar that I am hurting, that I need help, that I need healing—it is then that I am able to help somebody else find the way to a balm in Gilead.

I am walking in my chains, and I am not alone. Somebody else came in here walking in chains.

The church is growing today . . . but the preacher is walking in chains.

A church is on fire for God today . . . but the preacher is walking in chains.

Ask the preacher, "How are you doing?" More than likely, the preacher will tell you, "The Lord is blessing." But the truth is that the preacher is walking in chains.

Somebody else is here today with a load that is too heavy to carry back.

Somebody else is here nursing sores and licking wounds and trying to get free from something that is tying you up, and holding you back, and killing your spirit—that is walking in chains.

These chains represent my predicament. I am supposed to be a preacher, but here I am in bonds. Maybe the point of my bonds is that it is . . .

HARD TO BE ARROGANT IN CHAINS!

Scholarly arguments aside, do not forget that a man, who at one point in his life had much about which to be arrogant, wrote this word to the church at Ephesus. If you stood Paul up in the synagogue and asked him to introduce himself, he would tell you that he was . . .

Circumcised the eighth day
Of the stock of Israel,
Of the tribe of Benjamin, an Hebrew of the Hebrews;
As touching the law, a Pharisee;
Concerning zeal, persecuting the church;
Touching the righteousness which is in the law, blameless
(Philippians 3:5-6).

After all of that, after such a glowing self-introduction, Paul says all of that does not matter because now he is an ambassador in bonds.

And this is what I came to tell you today; whatever you do . . .

DON'T BELIEVE THE INTRODUCTION!

Preachers know what it is like to go from place to place, from city to city, pulpit to pulpit, and there is always somebody there with a glowing introduction. There is always somebody there to tell where you have been and what you have done. Don't you believe it!

There is always somebody there to tell what you have studied, the academic achievements you have made, and what paper you have on your wall. Don't believe it!

There is always somebody there to introduce the "grea-a-a-t Reverend Doctor," the "mannn of Gawd" who can walk on water, heal the sick, raise the dead, and turn water into wine. Whatever you do, don't believe it! If you look closely, there is nothing but chains. When Paul wrote to the church at Colossae, he got to the end and added this one little sentence: "Remember my bonds."

Never mind what I said about myself, remember my bonds.

Never mind what others said about me, remember my bonds.

Did I tell you it is hard to be arrogant in chains? When the testament of what you really are is so evident that folks cannot hear a word you are saying . . . it is hard to be arrogant in chains! I thought I ought to tell you that chains will take the arrogance out of you. The chains will stop you in your tracks from taking credit for anything.

The chains will teach you to say with humility: "I am crucified with Christ: nevertheless I live; yet not I, but Christ liveth in me" (Galatians 2:20).

It is hard to be arrogant in your chains.

I am searching for a reason for these chains. These chains represent my predicament. I am supposed to be the preacher, but here I am in bonds. I am supposed to be a preacher, but here I am in these chains. If there is a revelation on this Word, perhaps it is that . . .

THE CHAINS ARE THE POWER
FOR MY PREACHING!

Now then, if it is true that the chains represent the struggle in my life . . .

If it is true that chains represent the opposing force in my life. . .

If it is true that the chains represent my confrontation with spiritual adversaries . .

If it is true that my chains represent a sign of my conviction and guilt for my sins . . .

And if it is true the chains represent that which removes from me the temptation to be arrogant, then, above all else, in a strange and peculiar way, my chains become the power for my preaching.

I do not understand this predicament; but somehow the chains I bear are the credentials I must present in order to be qualified to preach. The chains I bear are my sign and symbol that I am experienced in "chainology," and that therefore I am qualified to preach.

This is why. Those who come to the church want to hear from

somebody who has been through something. The folk who come to church do not want to hear from somebody who had to come over a little bump in the road. They want to hear from somebody who has been up the rough side of the mountain.

When folks see you coming to pray for them, they do not want to hear from somebody who had a headache last week. They want somebody praying who has been there, done that. They want somebody praying that has been in the valley and stayed all day.

When folks hear you talking about preaching, they don't want to hear from somebody who has been in a little rain. They want to hear from somebody who has been in the storm so long! They want to hear from somebody who knows what it is to say, "The storm keeps on raging in my life."

When folks see you coming to the pulpit, they do not want to hear from somebody who had a little trouble last year. They want to hear from somebody who knows what it is to be in a circumstance that makes you want to holler and throw up both of your hands!

Do not despair over your chains. Your chains are your testimony that you are qualified to preach. It is about these chains! These chains represent my predicament. Honestly, I would rather pursue my calling without these chains. I have a social history that makes me recoil at the mere mention of chains. Nevertheless, here I am, confined by my chains. I am confined by a commitment I cannot escape. I am imprisoned by my passion for the very thing that puts me in my chains.

Paul says, Pray for me "that utterance may be given unto me, that I may open my mouth boldly, to make known the mystery of the gospel" (Ephesians 6:19).

The reality is that if Paul had just kept quiet, his sentence might not have been so severe. Listen, I have decided that if I must preach and, if I must be imprisoned by these chains, I will open my mouth boldly. God does not have time for preachers who will not preach. God does not have time for any half-backed, lackluster, willy-nilly, sugar-coated sermons. God does not have time for preachers who are too afraid to preach, too board controlled to preach, or too money controlled to handle the Word of God.

Paul said it to Timothy, "Preach the word; be instant in season, out of season; reprove, rebuke, exhort with all longsuffering and doctrine" (2 Timothy 4:2). If God has placed an anointment on your life, preach the word. If you are going to wear these chains, preach the word, preach the word, preach the word!

> I'm walking in my chains. I'm not what I ought to be.
> I'm not what I'm going to be, but thank God, I'm not what I used to be.
>
> I'm walking in my chains; but I walk by faith and not by sight.
>
> I'm walking in my chains. But I still believe that "The steps of a good man are ordered by the Lord: and he delighteth in his way" (Psalm 37:23).
>
> I'm walking in my chains, but I believe John was right: "If the Son therefore shall make you free, ye shall be free indeed" (John 8:36).
>
> I'm walking in my chains, but I still believe the Lord is the Spirit: and where the Spirit of the Lord is, there is liberty (2 Corinthians 3:17).
>
> I'm walking in my chains, and if I stumble or if I fall, God promised to send angels to bear me up in their hands lest I dash my foot against a stone (Psalm 91:12).
>
> I'm walking in my chains, and I'm walking up the rough side of the mountain, and I'm doing my best to make it in.

7

A SIMPLE SOLUTION
TO A COMPLEX PROBLEM

CAROLYN ANN KNIGHT

2 KINGS 5:1-14, KJV

S everal years ago the Atlanta University Center (AUC), of which the Interdenominational Theological Center (ITC) is a part, received a generous gift from the president of Microsoft. No matter our personal opinion about Bill Gates, we were glad to receive that $10 million, which was to be used to upgrade the computer operations at the AUC. For ITC, the gift meant that every faculty and staff person would have the latest in computer technology in their office. We would have the fastest CD-ROM drive available. We would have Internet and e-mail capabilities. We would be able to access the library catalog directly from our offices. We would be able to communicate with the registrar without walking down the hall. Students would be able to register for classes from their homes simply by entering their pass codes.

The process of installing this equipment brought an air mixed with excitement and anxiety to the campus. Those of us who were computer literate could not wait to get online on the job. Those of us who had been avoiding the computer like the plague knew that we could avoid these machines no longer. Me, I was (and am) somewhere in between. I do not know all that I want to know about computers, but I am a long way from being intimidated by them.

After the computers were installed, I was walking down the hall one day and noticed that one of my colleagues was sitting in front of her computer, just staring at it. Her face was perplexed, and there was a look of frustration on her brow. She asked me if I could be of any assistance. When I entered her office, I saw that her situation was indeed serious. After many attempts, she had not been able to even turn her computer on. I pushed the green "on" button, and nothing happened. I suggested that perhaps it had not been installed correctly. So we went about the business of undoing all of the cables and plugging them in where we thought they should be . . . nothing happened. So again, we undid all of the cables and put them back in their original positions . . . still, nothing happened. By this time, my face looked exactly like that of my colleague—perplexed and frustrated.

As we tried to figure out our next move, a passing student saw our despair and came to the rescue. He started where I had started, pushing the green "on" button. I thought to myself "Here we go again." But then he did something that neither my colleague nor I had done. He looked on the floor and saw that the computer was plugged into a power strip; however, the strip's red indicator light was not turned on, so the computer could not get power. The student bent down, turned on the power strip, and the computer came on—a simple solution to a complex problem.

The purpose of this sermon and the meaning of this text is to help us discover that solutions to problems in the new millennium, and the implementation of these methodologies, will come from simple people, in simple places, and in simple situations.

Author D. Elton Trueblood, a member of the Quaker religion, in *The Predicament of Modern Man*, writes that the biggest disappointment of the twentieth-century has been the fact that technological advances and scientific discoveries, as well as economic and political breakthroughs, have failed to make us a happier, healthier, more wholesome society.[1] Trueblood writes that as technology has advanced, morality has declined. As industry has skyrocketed, ethics and values have nose-dived. As economics have enjoyed a period of relative peace from military confrontation, spiritual war has been engaged. No doubt there is a crisis at hand. We cannot continue on this course. We live in a society that is unraveling. William Howe and Neil Strauss, in the book entitled *The Fourth Turning*, call this day in which we live "chaotic time."

We live in a world gone seriously awry and amuck. There exists in this land an ironic contrast between want and plenty. There is a widening gap between the haves and the have-nots, and the have-nots and the "have-even-lesses." We live in a nation of great economic disparity. Less than 10 percent of this nation's population controls the wealth of the land, while the remaining 90 percent has little or no demonstrable net worth. Get this: ill-tempered, bad-mannered, cross-dressing, gun-toting, neck-grabbing, spitting athletes make millions of dollars, while teachers and doctors can barely make ends meet, and preachers are criticized for the cars they drive and the clothes they wear.

Why is it that The Temptations, The Miracles, The Supremes, The Four Tops, Marvin Gaye, Stevie Wonder, and Martha and the Vandellas sang the same songs, in the same town, on the same record label, yet rappers like Tupac Shakur and the Notorious B.I.G. could not get along without killing one another, with one living on the East Coast and the other one on the West Coast?

We are losing our children and our young people. Children are dying before they really have a chance to live. Their futures are being destroyed. Their hopes are being dashed. They are dying long before they learn to drive. Far too numerous are the images of young people in handcuffs too large for their little wrists. In city after city, young people know how to fire a gun before they can really walk and chew gum at the same time. Persons in the fields of medicine and sociology tell us that we have a life expectancy of close to one hundred years, and yet teenage suicides have increased threefold in the last decade. Not only are babies having babies, but babies are also killing babies and themselves. Just this week, a seventeen-year-old tossed her baby into the river because she could not get a baby-sitter.

Eighty percent of this nation's high school students admit they have cheated on exams, and fifty percent say that they do not believe cheating is wrong. No wonder the President of this nation played golf last year with the National Collegiate Golf Champion from Arizona State. The young man reported that Clinton shot ninety, but wrote eighty-four on his scorecard. Michael J. Sandel writing in *Democracy's Discontent* and Robert J. Samuelson writing in *Good Life and Its Discontents* say that we are a depressed, worried, and unhappy nation.[2] There is a deep anguish in our nation and in its people. We long for a solution.

The daring scenario between Naaman and the prophet Elisha can be counted among the most dramatic in all of Old Testament literature. This text, though well known, is timely tailored to teach us that often life's most difficult problems and hardest circumstances can be remedied by simple solutions. Naaman, commander of the army of the king of Syria, was a great man. The record says that he was mighty in valor and that many battles had been won for his nation under his military might and strategic leadership. Naaman was a respected man in his community and held in the highest regard by everyone, including the king. He was a highly decorated soldier; he was a hero in his hometown; he was fearless in the face of battle. He was a competent and courageous captain; but he was a leper.

Naaman, commander of the army, was a leper.

Naaman, mighty man of valor, was a leper.

Naaman, a great and honorable man, was a leper.

It is important to note that Naaman's leprosy was not of the severest nature. It was not of the form that was associated in Old Testament times with sin and death. He was not ostracized by society. He was not relegated to a colony. He was not banished from the neighborhood. He was not sentenced to the asylum. He could lead his soldiers through the streets of Syria. He could be a husband to his wife and a father to his children. Naaman's leprosy was of a mild form. It had to be, or else he could not come in contact with the king. I was thinking about this whole issue of wholeness and healing while preparing this message, and

I thought that maybe wholeness in our lives ought to be an objective, but not necessarily the goal.

Naaman was a mighty man of valor, but life has a way of giving every one of us a humbling conjunction: smart girl, but . . . handsome brother, but . . . great professor, but . . . important leader, but . . . powerful preacher, but. This is a connecting conjunction to remind us that whatever our greatest assets are, there is something that detracts from them.

I am convinced that true wholeness rests in how we negotiate the conjunctions in our lives. It is important that Naaman did not let the conjunction in his life stop him from making a contribution to society. We must learn to negotiate the conjunctions in our lives. You do not have to have it all together, all the time, in all places before you can participate in humanity's struggle for peace, justice, righteousness, and truth. We must live with the conjunctions in our lives. Others have done it, you can, too. Handel was paralyzed, but he wrote the "Hallelujah Chorus." Beethoven was deaf, but he heard the melody of a "Ninth Symphony." Michelangelo was broke and depressed, but he still brought heaven inside the Sistine Chapel with a paintbrush. Fanny J. Crosby went blind at six weeks of age, but she wrote "Blessed Assurance." Wilma Rudolph had polio, but she could run like the wind. Naaman functioned in spite of his leprosy. He made a contribution. He was productive. We must learn to function with our conjunction.

On their many campaigns to raid and war with other nations on foreign soil, the armies of the Syrians would bring back boys and girls to serve as servants. One such girl found herself a servant for none other than Naaman's wife. She was privy to conversations between Naaman and his wife. She saw Naaman's condition. Even though she was a slave in Naaman's household, her spirit was free. She had retained in her spirit the God of the homeland. She had kept in her heart the rhythms of Almighty God. Even though she was miles away from her home, those rhythms still pulsated in her spirit. She was not at home but her faith was as strong as the rock of Gibraltar. She knew that

Naaman and his wife were reasonable people. She knew that they would not refuse any reasonable suggestion to cure Naaman's leprosy.

The text does not say how she broached the subject, but one day she said to her mistress, "If only Mr. Naaman could jet to the prophet in Israel he would cure him of his leprosy." Apparently, there was something in this young girl that made Naaman's wife take her advice and tell her husband. Naaman demonstrated the strength of his own character in taking that servant girl's advice. Even though he was the boss, Naaman recognized that he did not know everything. Even though Naaman was in charge, he still could receive advice from this servant girl. No matter who you are in life, you can always learn from somebody else. Politicians need to listen to the people; adults need to listen to their children; men need to listen to women; employers need to listen to employees; pastors should listen to members, and professors need to listen to students.

Naaman took the servant girl's advice to the king, and he granted Naaman permission to go to his brother king in Israel for his cure. The king gave Naaman a letter requesting that the king of Israel do whatever was necessary to cure his commander of leprosy. Naaman took gifts to show his appreciation and gratitude for anything done on his behalf and headed toward Israel.

Once in Israel, Naaman presented his letter to the king. Immediately the king tore his clothes in frustration and despair. He said that he was not a god to make people live or die. He asked the question "Why is the king of Syria trying to start a fight with me by sending this man to me?" The problem here is that although Naaman followed the advice of the servant girl, he misunderstood her instructions. She did not tell Naaman to go to the king of Israel. She told him to go to the prophet of Israel. When Elisha, the man of God, heard that the king was upset, he sent for Naaman. Then the commander would know that there is a prophet in Israel. Elisha was saying, "Naaman, you went to the king, but you are really looking for the King of kings."

When Naaman and his entourage, horses, chariots, and

attendants arrived at the home of Elisha, he was told by the prophet's messenger "Go wash seven times in the Jordan River and he will be cured of his leprosy."

That's it! Go wash seven times in the Jordan, and you will be cured of your leprosy. Hold on here! Wait one minute! This was not proper protocol. This was unacceptable! No formal introduction between the captain and the prophet . . . no greeting . . . no handshake . . . just a simple list of instructions delivered by a lowly emissary. This was not how things should be done. Naaman was an important man with a critical condition. Enraged, Naaman stormed away from the prophet's house fuming and complaining that he did not come all that way just to be told to wash in the muddy waters of the Jordan. If he wanted to go wash in the river, the rivers of Damascus, Abanah, and Pharpar were far better and more beautiful than the Jordan. Pouting, Naaman said, "I thought he would have at least come out to me and waved his hand, said some words and effected a cure. I was expecting hocus-pocus! I wanted some shenanigans! I wanted some fireworks! I wanted some complicated formula. I wanted some abstract principle! I wanted some difficult ritual! This is an insult! This is an outrage!"

Naaman's attendants showed greater wisdom than their master. They ran after Naaman and pleaded, "Father, if the man of God had told you some great thing to do, would you not have done it? Surely you can go and wash in the rivers of Damascus, but that is not where your healing can be found. Your healing is in the Jordan. You have been washing in the waters of Damascus all of your life, but you have not been cured."

Part of our problem, as we survey this sick situation that has saturated our society, is that we have been washing in rivers where there is no healing and no power. We have been associating and aligning ourselves with people who cannot help us. You can wash in political rivers if you want, but that is not where your healing can be found. You can wash in economic rivers if you want, but that is not where your healing can be found. You can wash in sexual rivers if you want, but that is not where your healing can be found. You can wash in the biggest river, the pretty river if you want, but that is not where your healing is.

"Captain Naaman, why not follow these simple instructions and go wash in the Jordan?" These simple lieutenants demonstrated that they knew far better than Naaman how the great God of the universe operates. They knew that there was a difference in God's way of doing things and our way of doing things. They knew that with God this complicated problem had a simple solution. There was no need for intensive care. This is not a case for the emergency room. Naaman, you do not need an organ transplant, or a heart-bypass, or a blood transfusion. You do not need oxygen or a respirator. Just go wash seven times in the Jordan and you will be clean.

"Naaman, it really is not the place or the prophet, it is the power of God. Naaman, go wash seven times in the Jordan."

It is important to note right here that despite Naaman's response to Elisha's instructions, the prophet's instructions did not change. God does not change divine requirements of us just because we do not like God's methods.

Naaman went, and with each dip in the Jordan, his leprosy began to disappear. The text does not tell us why he was told to dip seven times, instead of three, four, or five times. In Bible times, the number seven meant different things at different times. However, I do know that God requires total, complete, full and absolute obedience. We can follow God at a distance and be saved. We can pray sometimes and get healed. But we cannot serve only our church and truly be a disciple. We cannot water this thing down. This is a gospel without compromise. Allegiance to God must be total.

He went down one time and nothing happened . . . "Not one time, Naaman, seven times."

He went down two times and nothing happened . . . "Not two times, Naaman, seven times."

He went down three times, and nothing happened . . . "Not three times, Naaman, seven times."

He went down four times, and his skin began to tingle . . .

"Not four times, Naaman, seven times."

Don't be content to be a little healed, a little saved, a little blessed. Naaman went down for the fifth time and he felt something. "Not five times, Naaman, seven times."

He went down a sixth time—looked pretty good. "Not six times, Naaman, seven times."

Finally, after the seventh time, Naaman's skin was as smooth as a baby's bottom, and he was cleaned. He was made whole.

Naaman found his healing and the solution to his problem when he obeyed the word of God. Naaman went back to the prophet's house. This time, Elisha was standing in the doorway to greet Naaman. Naaman went back to offer payment for his healing, but Elisha refused. When God restores health and wholeness to a person, we cannot pay for it with money; but we can pay for it with service.

Martin Luther King Jr. said it, and I agree, "We have some difficult days ahead."[3] We've got a charge to keep, a God to glorify to serve this present age.[4] We've got an AIDS pandemic to cure

> a drug epidemic to root out
> a crime wave to tame
> a healthcare crisis to manage
> a homeless humanity to shelter
> an illiterate environment to weed out
> an ebonics mentality to understand
> rappers to reach
> a crop of geniuses to cultivate.

There are still restaurants that will not serve Oprah, and Danny Glover still cannot get a cab. There are streets that Will Smith cannot drive down, and courses that Tiger Woods cannot play. These situations are serious. These problems are complicated. But I believe now and always will believe that . . .

> where there is a will, there is a way;
> love is stronger than hate;
> right is better than wrong;
> action is better than inaction;
> a smile will destroy a frown;

a hug will beat a shove;
it is better to give than receive;
a job should come before marriage;
marriage should come before sex;
commitment should come before children;
the ballot is stronger than the bullet;
work is better than welfare;
truth is mightier than a lie;
hope will arrest despair;
Christ can defeat sin;
God is bigger than the devil; and
heaven is better than hell.

Whenever we have occasion to reflect on the life of our prophet, Martin Luther King Jr., whether it be in January on the anniversary of his birth, or in April on the date of his untimely death, we remember well how he stood on the steps of the Lincoln Memorial that hot August day in 1963 and told us of his dream for America. Dr. King told us that he had a dream that one day sons and daughters of slaves and former slave owners would be able to sit down at the table in fellowship and harmony; that little black boys and little black girls would one day be able to play with little white boys and little white girls; that one day blacks and whites would be able to get along together.

Well, I was seven years old when Dr. King articulated his dream. But today, I too, have a dream. My dream is a little different than Dr. King's dream; however, I really believe that if we are serious about Martin King's dream, then we must be serious about my dream.

I have a dream that one day little black boys and little black girls will play together.

I have a dream that one day blacks will be able to get along together.

I have a dream that one day black men and black women will be able to get along together.

I have a dream that one day black women will be able to get along together.

I have a dream that one day black churches and black businesses will be able to get along together.

I have a dream that one day black preachers and black politicians will be able to get along together.

I have a dream that one day young people and not so young people in the black community will be able to get along together.

I have a dream that one day male preachers and female preachers will be able to get along together.

Wait, wait, wait, I have a dream that one day it will not matter if the preacher is male or female—just as long as they preach the Word in season and out of season—just as long as they preach the Word . . .

> until men and women coming running crying "What must
> I do to be saved?"
> until demons tremble;
> until governments are toppled;
> until lame people walk, and blind people see;
> until every knee bows and every tongue confesses that
> Jesus is Lord to the glory of God, the Father.

So walk together, children; pray together, children; love together, children; work together, children. There is a great camp meeting in the Promised Land! All it takes is simple obedience. The most complicated problems require simple solutions.

Time is filled with swift transition.
Naught on earth unmoved can stand.
Build your hopes on things eternal.
Hold to God's unchanging hand.
When your journey is completed,
If to God you have been true,
Fair and bright your home in glory,
Your enraptured soul will view.
Hold to His hand, to God's unchanging hand.
Hold to His hand, to God's unchanging hand.
Build your hopes on things eternal.
Hold to God's unchanging hand.[5]

NOTES

1. D. Elton Trueblood, *The Predicament of Modern Man* (New York: Harper & Brothers, 1944).

2. Michael J. Sandel, *Democracy's Discontent* (Cambridge: Harvard University Press, 1997) and Robert J. Samuelson, *Good Life and Its Discontents* (New York: Vintage Books, 1997).

3. "I've Been to the Mountaintop," speech delivered on April 3, 1968, in Memphis, Tennessee.

4. "A Charge to Keep I Have," lyrics by Charles Wesley. Public domain.

5. "Hold to God's Unchanging Hand," lyrics by Jennie Wilson. Public domain.

8

RESPONDING TO THE MACEDONIAN CALL

WALTER MALONE

ACTS 16:6-10, KJV

The story of our text is centered around the second missionary journey of the apostle Paul. This journey would mark a distinct transition in the ministry of this outstanding missionary, for Paul and Barnabas had parted company over the issue of John Mark. Since Paul had refused to allow Mark to be a part of this second missionary journey, Barnabas took Mark and sailed to Cyprus. Paul had chosen a new partner by the name of Silas, and they went through Syria and Cilicia.

When Paul and Silas came to Derbe and Lystra, a young man named Timothy joined them. Timothy would become a son in the ministry to Paul, and through the years he would prove to be an invaluable resource to the apostle's ministry. As they continued on this second missionary journey, Paul desired to go to the Roman province of Asia and preach the gospel. He felt that Asia should be the next focus for their mission; however, the Holy Spirit said "No." With the door of Asia closed by the Holy Spirit, Paul and his companions headed north to preach throughout the Phrygian and Galatian territories. When they came to the border of Mysia, they wanted to go northeast and share the good news in the area of Bithynia. But Luke reveals that again the Holy Spirit refused them. So Paul and his missionary team passed by Mysia and came down to Troas.

It is both interesting and inspirational to note that Paul's itinerary was not God's itinerary. But when the Holy Spirit revealed God's plan for their journey to Paul, at that moment the apostle was willing to succumb his will to God. I believe that in this contemporary hour churches would do well to recognize the relationship between reason and revelation. For what is on our agenda does not always match God's agenda. We need to be flexible enough to make the necessary adjustments, both in life and in ministry, as the Spirit of God directs us.

The reason that the Spirit of God would not allow Paul to go to the Roman province of Asia at that time was made plain at Troas. There a vision appeared to Paul in the night. A man of Macedonia stood before him saying, "Come over to Macedonia and help us" (v. 9, NIV).

It is here that we come to the heart of the text. Paul and his companions responded to the Macedonian call with a sense of commitment to God and concern for others. Luke records, "After [Paul] had seen the vision, immediately we endeavoured to go into Macedonia, assuredly gathering that the Lord had called us for to preach the gospel unto them" (v. 10).

The church today still is receiving a Macedonian call. From every city in our nation there is a cry going out, "Come over here! We need help in Macedonia." What a devastating contrast of development and destruction characterizes the cities of our country! From one perspective we see progress, success, economic development, educational stability, and community investment. But from another perspective we see failure, racism, social injustice, poor education, hunger, and an oppressed community. In every city, the church today is still receiving a Macedonian call.

Some young person who is involved in drugs and gang activity—not because he loves it, but because he does not want to be left out of the crowd—is ready to become his own person in Christ. Some pilgrim in pain has kept constant company with misery and misfortune and is ready for someone to tell her that there is a balm in Gilead. Some drug-addicted man who has been taking cocaine to get high, barbiturates to get low, and using alcohol as a buffer in between is ready to become responsible for his life. Some middle-class or upper-class woman has discovered, like the rich young ruler, that money won't make her happy, and she is ready to reprioritize her life.

There is a call to the church from Macedonia: "Come over here! We need help in Macedonia." And so the question that confronts us today is the same one that faced Paul, How will we respond to the Macedonian call?

Many contemporary churches are failing to respond rightly to the Macedonian call. They are failing because they have allowed their religion to become a mere social affair. They enter into the sanctuary on Sunday morning with a false sense of moralism, and feel as though they have done God a favor by showing up. Church for them is equated with entertainment. They come to church to see the choir perform, and to watch the preacher execute some pulpit gymnastics. After the benediction, they go home and become so stale in their religion that they lose sensitivity to the hurts of a broken society. This failure also can be attributed to the absence of a vital Christian education ministry in the life of the church.

Where there is the absence of teaching, there will be people who misunderstand the church's ministry and purpose.

Where there is the absence of teaching, people will not have their minds stimulated theologically.

Where there is the absence of teaching, people will not be equipped for the work of ministry.

Where there is the absence of teaching, there will not be an emphasis on discipleship training.

Dietrich Bonhoeffer rightly declared in his book *The Cost of Discipleship*, "Christianity without the living Christ is inevitably Christianity without discipleship, and Christianity without discipleship is always Christianity without Christ."[1]

The contemporary church needs to respond appropriately to the Macedonian call. Therefore, I want to submit two aspects of Paul's spiritual life as a proper perspective for responding to the Macedonian church's call.

In the first place, Paul responded to the Macedonian call because of his love for God. On one occasion Paul spoke of himself as a servant, or bond slave, of Jesus Christ. And on another occasion he said, "I am crucified with Christ: nevertheless I live; yet not I, but Christ liveth in me: and the life which I now live in the flesh I live by the faith of the Son of God, who loved me, and gave himself for me" (Galatians 2:20). Paul really loved the Lord. His deepest desire was that God would have complete control of his life. His constant prayer was that God's perfect will would be manifested in his ministry. So when the Spirit of God refused to allow the apostle to go to Bithynia, but instead said "Go to Macedonia," Paul did not mind submitting his will to God's will because he loved the Lord.

If you and I really love the Lord, if we love the Lord with heart, mind, soul, and strength, we will not resist responding to the Macedonian call. The Christian life is a constant submission of our will to God's will. Remember, Jesus said, "Seek ye first the kingdom of God, and his righteousness . . ." (Matthew 6:33). Also recall that he said, "Whosoever will come after me, let him deny himself, and take up his cross, and follow me" (Mark 8:34).

The question that always stares us in the face is this: What is our ultimate concern? Is our ultimate concern to build personal sandcastles, or is our ultimate concern to help usher in the kingdom of God? As one gives one's life to Christ and grows in spiritual maturity, the less one ought to be concerned with earthly matters and the more concerned one ought to be with eternal matters. My ultimate concern is that God's will be worked out in my life, so every now and then I find myself praying:

Use me, Lord, in thy service,
Draw me nearer everyday.

I am willing, Lord, to run all the way.
If I falter while I'm trying,
Don't be angry, let me stay.
I am willing, Lord, to run all the way.
Pain of heart once scorned by loved ones,
Just a little sunshine now and then.
There are mountains in my life so hard to climb.
But I promise to keep on climbing,
If you only let me in.
I'm willing, Lord, to run on all the way.

In the second place, Paul responded to the Macedonian call because of his love for people. It was to the Christians at Rome that Paul said, "Brethren, my heart's desire and prayer to God for Israel is, that they might be saved" (Romans 10:1). To the Christians at Corinth the apostle said, "Ye are our epistle written in our hearts, known and read of all men" (2 Corinthians 3:2). The apostle Paul had weaknesses and failures in life just like all other persons. But one of the outstanding characteristics of his life was that he loved people. He wanted to see the best manifested in people. He wanted others to have a saving relationship with Jesus Christ.

Our Christianity must be expressed on both the vertical and horizontal planes. We must have a love that reaches up to God, but we also must have a love that reaches out to humanity. God does not want us to be sympathetic saints, but rather compassionate Christians. We ought to have a love for people that moves us to respond to the Macedonian call. A love for people constrains us to witness to the lost. A love for people moves us to feed the hungry, cloth the naked, and house the homeless. A love for people mandates that we seek to liberate those who are in oppressive communities.

Martin Luther King Jr. once said, "The ultimate measure of a man is not where he stands in moments of comfort and convenience, but where he stands at times of challenge and controversy. The true neighbor will risk his position, his prestige, and even his life for the welfare of others. In dangerous valleys and hazardous pathways, he will lift some bruised and beaten brother to a higher and more noble life."[2]

NOTES
1. Dietrich Bonhoeffer, *The Cost of Discipleship* (New York: MacMillan Publishing Company, Inc., 1960), 63-64.
2. Martin Luther King Jr., *The Words of Martin Luther King, Jr.* (New York: Newmarket Press, 1983), 24.

9

WALKING IN ORDERED STEPS

TRINETTE V. McCRAY

PSALM 119:133; MATTHEW 14:28, KJV

I n Psalm 119:133 we find David's prayer—the only time we find this particular prayer of David in the Bible. David lifts up his voice to God and says, "Order my steps in your word and let not any iniquity have dominion over me." That's from the King James Version, but in Today's English Version we find it reads, "As you have promised, keep me from falling. Don't let me be overcome by evil."

Now moving to Matthew's Gospel, the fourteenth chapter and the twenty-eighth verse, we find these words of Peter: "Bid me to come to thee on the water." But I like the way it reads in the TEV: "Order me, Jesus, order me to come out on the water to you."

I want to lay upon this text these words: Walking in Ordered Steps. Well, I've also been inspired to suggest this as the sermon title: Ordered Steps, yet Failing Faith. Either of these titles may suit our need at this particular time—or at any other time!

I hear Minister Sabrina Watson-Smith say, "We can get so caught up in information that we neglect our formation." We can get so caught up in wanting to help that we forget that we also *need* help. We can get so focused on pointing at the ills of the world that we can get shortsighted about our own ills. And so as we are forming ourselves as ministers of the gospel, it behooves us to take a moment to allow God's light from God's lighthouse to shine upon us and come into our hearts and into our souls, and to shine into the deepest corners of our existence, which we keep hidden from others but can't keep hidden from the Lord.

Shine on, Lord. Shine your light into our closets, shine into our cupboards, and if you find anything that shouldn't be, O Lord, call it to our attention and let your Holy Spirit call it from our lips. We want to be right. We want to be saved. We want to be whole.

We have to watch out because we are walking in ordered steps. But even ordered steps can have a failing faith. We have Psalm 119. This psalm is not like any other psalm. It seems to be a collection of David's sporadic prayers and utterances and requests to God. It's a long psalm that calls us to evaluate periodically the condition of our souls. An unevaluated, unmonitored soul is an open invitation to evil and corruption. In his prayer, David makes note of his conversation to God as he engages and encounters life. It would behoove us to keep a conversation going with God as *we* encounter and are engaged in this life. I heard somebody say "I'd rather *see* a sermon than *hear* one any day." God's people need to be persons who live in communion with God. How can they trust that what we preach is from God if we have not stopped somewhere beside the shore to listen for the Lord?

This psalm is left to us as a record of the fact that David maintained contact with God. David communed with God at every turn. You see we might graduate from seminary, but we will never graduate from communing with God. I love that song by Cleavant Derricks that invites us to "have a little talk with Jesus."[1] Just a little talk with Jesus makes everything all right.

What some have said about this psalm is that it will either warm you or it will shame you. You will read this psalm and you will either feel pretty good about the condition of your soul, or you will cry out, "O Lord, it is I!" Here in verse 133, David prays for God's goodwill to be showered upon him. David prays to God, "Order my steps." In other words David prays, "Having led me into the right way, let every step I take in that way be under the guidance of thy grace." I would like to say it this way: It isn't enough to get started walking in God's way. You'd better pray, like David, to continue in that way. "Many they are who start in the race; But with the light they refuse to keep pace; Others accept it because it is new, but not very many expect to go through."[2] Some have come to ministry because it was a new thing, just like any other new thing. But they will not keep pace when the going gets rough and the going gets tough. "Not very many expect to go through."

In his prayer, David was sincere, true, and one who desired "to go through." But there's more to David. David, a man destined to be king. David, a musician who tames the raging spirit by the strumming of the harp strings. David, a compassionate man. David, a praying man. David, even David, a man after God's own heart. The David we know was acquainted with failing. The King James Version says, "Order my steps," but the Good News Version says, "Keep me from falling." David knew that he walked in a land of slips and stumbles and slippery slopes that lead down the path of lost hopes. David knew that, no matter how hard he tried, he could stumble and fall. It doesn't matter how close we are to God; falling could be just a day away—just a day away if we don't pray the devil away!

I'm talking about *prayer* though. I'm not talking about "Now I lay me down to sleep, I pray the Lord my soul to keep." I'm talking about *prayer*—Holy Ghost, Pentecostal, sanctified, true and tried prayer. I'm talking about prayer that causes beads of sweat to fall from your brow. Prayer that causes the earth to tremble and shake. Prayer that will wake up the sleeping and shake up the dead. I'm talking about prayer—world-changing prayer, soul-saving prayer, demon-defeating prayer, shackle-breaking prayer, clothe-the-naked prayer, prisoner-releasing prayer. I'm talking about *prayer*.

Ordered steps was only half of David's prayer. He went on to say, "Let not any iniquity have dominion over me." In other words, David said "Don't let me be overcome by evil." Don't miss the message here. David didn't pray "I won't let me be overcome by evil." David prays to God, "Don't let me. . . ." It seems to me, if he had said "I won't let" that would mean he could walk in his own power, that he could walk in his own mind, that he could walk in his own steps. But David wasn't crazy, you see. David knew his own limitations. David knew that he was limited in overcoming evil all by himself.

I'm talking about *evil*—ambitious evil, self-absorbed evil, ungrateful evil, jealous evil. Unrighteous, lying, stealing, and cheating evil. I'm-gonna-get-you-before-you-get-me evil. David knew his limitations. So David didn't pray "I won't let" because David knew what he was capable of if he were to walk only in his own power and might. David prayed to God, "Don't let." You see, here David showed he was wise enough to know that the only power that is great enough, the only one who is strong enough, the only army that is big enough to hold back that manipulating, undercutting, slick and slimy, tripping and trifling evil one is God. "God," David said, "call upon your angels and don't let. God, send down warring angels and don't let. Send down delivering angels and don't let. Send down fire, Lord, and don't let. Hold back the water and don't let. God, don't let." You see, David knew that we do have limitations, and David knew about his own limitations.

But, even as much as Moses stuttered, Miriam gossiped, Jacob lied, Rachel stole, Noah got drunk, David had an affair, Hosea married a prostitute, Naomi was widowed, Abraham was old and Sarah was old too, Jeremiah was young, Elijah was burned out, Thomas doubted, Peter was quick-tempered, Martha was a worrywart, and John the Baptist was weird—God used them all in a very special way. Alienated by circumstances, estranged by mishaps, even inasmuch as they had limitations, God ordered their steps. God will call and God will use whomever God will. God will order the steps of those who have limitations.

So here we have David's prayer. But David's prayer in the Old Testament becomes Peter's plea in the New Testament. "Order" meant "keep" for David, but "order" will mean "Call for, Jesus" for

Peter. A call from Jesus is a guarantee that you will be kept. If Jesus calls you, Jesus will keep you—he'll keep you by the power of God.

In Matthew 14:22-33, we find the disciples in the boat on the water in the midst of the storm. Peter and the other disciples were in the boat when they saw Jesus walking on the water far off across the sea. Peter, quick-lipped Peter, pleads with Jesus to call him out of the boat.

Haven't we, like Peter, been quick to say "Lord, call me. Lord, use me. Lord, send me. Lord, I'll serve you until the end of my days. Lord, just give me a place somewhere in your kingdom. It doesn't matter to me where; it doesn't matter to me what. Lord, call me." Some of us have been quick-lipped like Peter. But Peter's life in the boat must have been a can't-stand-it-in-here-any-longer kind of experience. You know what happens when you get that can't-stand-it-in-here-any-longer kind of feeling. We will say anything to God, if God will get us out of this can't-stand-it-in-here-any-longer experience. Some of us today are where we are because we had a can't-stand-it-in-here-any-longer kind of experience.

Just think about it. Why else would a person in his right mind walk on water rather than stay in the safety and security of the boat—except that he has had a can't-stand-it-in-here-any-longer kind of experience. Perhaps Peter saw more . . . a more powerful possibility, a surer security, a miraculous ministry, and a better traveling companion on the water than he had found in the boat. But I want to ask Peter a question: Peter, why didn't you stay in the boat? Peter, you know about water. Why would you do that, Peter? Why didn't you stay in the boat?

I can hear Peter saying, "I couldn't stay in that boat any longer. Do you know who was in that boat? I mean, just think about it. I saw Jesus, and then I looked around and I saw who I'd been in the boat with. I looked and I saw doubting Thomas, doubting all the time; jealous James, jealous all the time; I saw meticulous Matthew and gypping Judas and quick-tempered me. I knew I couldn't stay in that boat any longer!"

There are some folks in our boats that we need to get away from. Our longing causes us to say to Jesus, "Call for me, Jesus. I can't stay in this boat any longer!" Like Peter, we realize there are doubting folks in our boat, jealous folk in our boat, quick-tempered folk in our boat, envious folk in our boat. Wrapped-up, tangled-up, and tied-up folks are in this boat. And like Peter, we've got to decide that we are getting out of the boat.

I hear Peter saying that, and then when I think about it, I know I'd rather follow Jesus, too. I'll follow Jesus. I don't care where Jesus is. If Jesus is flying, I'd rather fly with Jesus. You know, Jesus is a far better traveling companion than anyone else we know. Peter, looking out on the horizon, sees a familiar figure whom he believes to be Jesus. He begins to sense that I-want-to-be-where-you-are kind of feeling coming over him again. But Peter didn't have anything to worry about. Why would he worry? He should have known that his steps had been ordered a long time ago. And my sisters and brothers, why should we worry? Don't we know that our steps, too, have been ordered a long time ago?

Whether to move out with Jesus should not be a question. Wherever Jesus calls us to go and however Jesus calls us to move should not be anything to agonize over. There should be no need to think about it or to take time to digest the idea. We ought to go right away because we know that we already walk in ordered steps.

The Lord ordered my steps a long time ago. It wasn't just when I was called into the ministry. No, the Lord ordered my steps as I was in my mother's womb. The Lord ordered my steps when I was a baby. As my parents and godparents stood in the presence of God, dedicating my life to the Lord, my steps were ordered. Peter should have known that God told Jeremiah that he was known before he was in his mother's womb. Why would Peter have a care? Jesus had already told him that we would be central in the building up of the church. Why would Peter have a care?

Jesus called Peter, you see, from the shallow existence of the boat to a new life in the deep. And that's what Jesus is calling us to. When we talk about vital ministries, vital ministries are in the deep. Jesus is calling us from the shallow existence of the boat to new life in the deep.

Well, Peter was thinking now with his foot on the edge of the boat. Can't you see Peter with his foot on the edge of that boat? He's thinking, Now I see Jesus and I see y'all. Look at Peter. There is no one else with a foot on the edge of the boat. Don't you know that sometimes we start out and look behind to see if anyone is coming with us? As we step back and reconsider our step, we call out to the others, "Y'all not coming?" Their indecision makes us check ourselves. Maybe there's something wrong with me, we think. I've got my foot on the edge of the boat. Can't you hear the thoughts of Peter while he has his foot there? He's thinking, Well, God delivered Daniel from the lion's den, Jonah from the belly of the whale, Shadrach, Meshach, and Abenego from the fiery furnace, so why wouldn't God deliver me?

Peter, then, with his foot on the edge of the boat, says to Jesus, "Jesus, order me to come out to you on the water. Jesus, call me and I will come." Jesus meets Peter's request. You got to be careful because your steps have already been ordered. Once you say to Jesus, "Call for me," Jesus immediately says "Come." Jesus doesn't have to think about it. Jesus doesn't have to call a committee meeting. Jesus doesn't need the council to come together. Jesus doesn't wait for the next board meeting. Jesus says, "If you want to come, then right now I order you to come—out of the boat and onto the water with me." Jesus said to Peter, "Come." Jesus calls to you and to me to come out on the water if we're willing to come. There's nothing stopping us from coming. Don't let the boat stop you from coming; don't let your companions stop you from coming; don't let the water stop you from coming. Jesus says, "Come!"

You see, *come* is one of Jesus' favorite expressions. "*Come* unto me all who are weary and heavy laden, and I will give you rest." "Whosoever will *come* after me, let him deny himself and take up his cross." "If anyone will *come* after me." "Suffer the little children to *come* unto me." We don't have to worry about Jesus' answer when he comes to us. Jesus says, "Come." Come.

Peter indeed had ordered steps. But Peter also had failing faith. Having failing faith is like having cement blocks tied to your feet, a five-hundred-pound weight strapped around your shoulders. Failing faith will take you down when you're trying to go up. You can't walk on water with failing faith. Failing faith will steal your attention from Jesus and focus it on the circumstances around you. Peter had ordered steps but failing faith. He was out on the water, too far from the boat to turn back. We, like Peter, have already stepped away from the boat. We're too far out here now, and we can't go back. We've come too far to turn around, too far to change our minds, too far to go back to what we used to do. We're out here now, and we have to make up our minds about which way we are going to go. We're out here now, and usually that's just when the winds begin to pick up.

Look at Peter now that he's out there. He hears the winds pick up. Their sound gets louder and louder. Winds like voices saying, "Look at you, Peter. You can't accomplish that. Look at you, Peter. You're out here all by yourself. Look at you, Peter. We're not going to help you. You're in some trouble now, Peter!" Those voices come to us when we are trying to get out of the boat, voices that say, "You're nobody. Who do you think you are? Look at you, short, round, female. Who would call you to preach? Look at you! You've got yourself into something now!"

I know what Peter felt like. I know what he felt like out there on the water. For the past several months, I've had some folks come to me with their winds. Discouraging winds, winds of despair, winds of hopelessness, winds of impossibilities. Winds, blowing winds. Winds, contrary winds, doubtful winds, lying winds, meddling winds, two-faced winds, stab-you-in-the-back winds, smiling-in-your-face-all-the-while-trying-to-take-your-place winds! We can't walk in the deep while we are paying attention to those winds! Jesus says to each of us, "I have ordered your steps. I will keep your feet. I will hold you up. I will still the waters. I will quiet the winds. I will fight your battles. I will keep you from falling." Jesus says, "Come."

I close with a story about a little girl, a little girl who lived in South Florida. She loved hot summer days when she could get out back and go into the river to swim. One such day she was so eager to get out and swim, she ran out wearing just her shorts and a top. She jumped from the pier into the water and began swimming away from the pier, farther into the river. But as she was swimming, her mother was looking out at her from the window. Up ahead in the river, the mother could see an alligator that had taken notice of her daughter and that had begun swimming toward the girl as she was swimming farther into the deep.

That mother ran from the window outside to the pier and from there yelled to her daughter, "Baby, turn around! Come toward me!" The daughter responded to her mother's call, making a U-turn and swimming back toward her mother. Kneeling down at the edge of the pier, the mother reached out her hands and grabbed her daughter as the girl reached the pier. But it was too late. The alligator had also reached the child and caught hold of her legs. There was the biggest tug-of-war you have ever seen in your life. The alligator was strong, but the mother was persistent. She was passionate and determined to save her child. So the mother dug her nails into her daughter's arms and pulled and tugged. A farmer responded to that mother's cries for help and came running to assist, finally retrieving the daughter from the grasping jaws of the alligator.

Well, the alligator had done quite a bit of damage to that child. She was in the hospital for three months. The doctors reconstructed her legs and healed her wounds. When it was time to go back to school, the daughter returned, and of course, everyone wanted to see her scars from the summer. They said to her, "I heard the alligator got hold of you. Let us see the scars on your legs." So the little girl pulled up her pant legs so the other children could see what the alligator had done, but she said to them, "Don't worry about those scars on my legs. I want you to see my arms. I want you to see the scars on my arms. These scars say my mother loved me and she wouldn't let me go. These are the scars of a mother's love. She dug her nails into me and she wouldn't let me go. These scars say that my mother loves me; she wouldn't turn me loose. My mother wouldn't lose me to that alligator. Look at these scars. These are the scars of love. Don't focus on the scars of life. See the scars of love."

My sisters and my brothers, God is calling to you. God will hold on to you, and God will not turn you loose. Show the scars of love that prove that God has laid God's hands on you and that God would not turn you loose. God will not lose you to the deep. We have ordered steps, so walk on in ordered steps. Walk on through the winds. Walk on through the storms. Walk on through the doubts, and walk on through the discouragement. Walk on through the opposition. Do what God has called you to do because you have ordered steps, not a failing faith.

NOTES

1. "Just a Little Talk with Jesus," lyrics by Cleavant Derricks. Copyright by The Stamps-Baxter Music & Ptg. Co. All rights reserved.

2. "I'm Going through Jesus." Public domain.

10
SAME NO MORE

VASHTI MURPHY McKENZIE

ACTS 3:1-10, KJV

Beloved, sometimes we live with the mistaken impression that things will always be the same. We will be in the same place, doing the same things, meeting the same challenges, contending with the same issues, wrestling with the same problems, worrying with the same worries, stressing the same stresses, toting the same barge, and lifting the same bale. Sometimes we live with the mistaken impression that things will always be the same.

We may want things to change, but we will not do anything to change them. There comes a point when same is what we want. It does not matter whether that same is positive or negative, same provides a certain amount of security. We know exactly what to expect. We know exactly what to experience, because it is the same. Same not only provides security, but it also provides comfort. It is comforting to know that same is going to be the same. There is no discomfort about same becoming worse or better. There is no discomfort about the rightness or wrongness, oughtness or shouldness, because it is the same. Same has a track record with us. It has been the same for a long time. Same is a familiar member of the family. Same works with us on the same job. Same employs us and signs our same check. Same lives with us in the same house. Same sleeps in the guest bedroom. Same eats at our table, spends our money, and like an unwelcome guest, same refuses to leave home.

Same has a track record with us. We have a scrapbook on same with all the same pictures in it. We have learned how to monitor same. We have put a homing device on same. We have tilled the same soil and planted the same seeds. We have learned how to do the same projects and the same assignments. We have cultivated same. We have nurtured same in our lives to the point that anything that is remotely different from same gets us upset because . . . it is not the same.

Anything that is not the same throws us off course. We become confused and lost when change replaces same. We break out into a cold sweat. Upset and aggravated does not begin to describe us when things are not the same.

In fact, some people get mad when something is not the same. Let someone do something different and watch all the members of the "same committee" move into action. Watch the committee protest against change because . . . things are not the same. Just let some innovation sneak in. Let a new idea move aboard and watch the "same patrol" go into action. If something out of the ordinary occurs, everybody will start going to "Same Anonymous" meetings, saying "Hi, my name is _____ and I am a 'sameaholic.' "

We live under the mistaken impression that things always will be the same. We stop looking for anything else. Our minds stagnate. Our energy is defeated. No new ideas in and no new ideas out. Innovation is dead and buried. We stop thinking. Creative thoughts do not stand a chance. Alternative directions are never considered. Ingenuity is devastated. Thinking outside of the box never crosses our minds—all because we live with the mistaken impression that things will always be the same.

Now, before anyone gets the wrong idea, same is a good and valuable member of the community. Same sits at the table with diversity and variety. Same has some redeeming value and worth. In fact, I have been married to the same man for many years and

I am not looking for a change. He is, however, not the same man that I married; and I am not the same woman that he walked up the aisle. The challenges of living in the 21st century have left an indelible imprint upon our lives. Crisis has deepened our faith. Struggle has strengthened our character and conviction. Our uniqueness as a couple has emerged in the midst of our own individuality. We are not the same.

The issue of living with the expectation that things will always be the same rises to the surface in the pericope found in Acts 3:1-10. The Book of Acts deals with the spreading of the gospel under the leadership of Peter first, and then under Paul. The church is birthed fifty days after the Resurrection on the day we call Pentecost. It is the day when the Holy Spirit was poured out among all flesh. The church spreads from a national concern to an international entity. The followers of Christ were empowered by the Holy Spirit to become witnesses, first in Jerusalem, Judea, Samaria, and to the uttermost parts of the world. It began with the Israelites and expanded to the Gentiles.

Many scholars attribute Acts to a man named Luke. He is perhaps the only Gentile biblical writer. Luke never walked with Christ. He did not see firsthand the miracles of the loaves and fish. Luke was not there when the water turned into wine at the wedding in Cana. He was not there when Christ hung on the cross, nor was he there when the Savior rose from the grave.

There is evidence, however, that he was a close friend and traveling companion of Paul. Some scholars conclude that some of Paul's doctrine is evident in the Gospel of Luke, as well as in the Acts of the Apostles. Paul calls Luke "the beloved physician" in Colossians 4:14. In Philemon 24, Luke is called Paul's fellow worker. In 2 Timothy 4:11, Luke was with Paul in the hours approaching Paul's death. Luke, as well as Mark, were companion workers. There is an indication of the personal use of the pronouns "we" and "they" in the later portion of Acts. Luke was with Paul in the early part of his second missionary journey, and again six years later at Philippi at the close of his third missionary journey. Luke was with Paul during his imprisonment of two years in Caesarea and two years in Rome.

In other words, Luke had time during Paul's prison sojourn to get firsthand data and accurate information from Paul and the other first founders of the church. Luke's scientific background prepared him to gather information in an orderly fashion. There were details important to Luke that Matthew and Mark did not include. In fact, Luke has one-half of the Lord's complete biography that the other Gospel writers did not include.

It may be possible that while he was in Jerusalem, Luke spent time with Mary, the earthly mother of Jesus. Perhaps it was in a conversation that Mary revealed what she had kept in her heart about the miraculous birth of the Christ. It could have been there that he learned about the shepherds. Maybe it was at Mary's feet that he learned about the angels singing in heaven. Mary could have told him of the angel bearing the news of a birth without human conception. Or Luke could have even learned it from James, the brother of Christ, the bishop of all of Jerusalem.

Many of the greatest hymns of the church are written from Luke's Gospel: "Ave Maria," or the words of the angel to Mary; "The Magnificat," or Mary's song; "The Benedictus" of Zachariah: and, the "Gloria in excelsis Deo" the heavenly angels sing.

In any case, the Holy Spirit used Luke to leave for us the Acts of the Apostles, or as some call it, the Acts of the Holy Spirit. Our text indicates that it is prayer time and Peter and John, two of the apostles, were on their way to prayer meeting. They saw a lame man sitting at a gate called Beautiful; what some scholars believe was the East gate of Jerusalem. It was called Beautiful because it was decorated with Corinthian bronze, and when the sun rose it cast a glorious glow upon the gate. There are two things in this passage of Scripture that capture our immediate attention. The first is the seriousness of the man's illness; the second is the immediacy of the cure. The man at the gate had been lame from birth. The man had a congenital condition that was constant and consistent. His condition rendered him helpless. He was forced to sit in the same place begging the same alms from whomever was going into and out of the temple to pray.

Every morning it would be the same thing—the lame man waited for somebody to carry him to the gate. Every day it was the same—he begged for alms from passersby. Every night it was the same—he waited for somebody to remember that he was at the gate and carry him home. He may have lived with the mistaken impression that things would always be the same.

In *Their Eyes Were Watching God*, Zora Neal Hurston wrote about a woman named Janey who was in the same position—living with the mistaken impression that things always would be the same.[1] Zora described Janey as being in a rut. The same thing kept happening and she was stuck in a rut. There was good ground underneath, but the wheels kept rolling over that good ground, pressing it down. When you live with the mistaken impression that things will always be the same, you will end up in a rut. There is good ground where you are. There is good opportunity, potential and substance, but same keeps rolling over you, and you live stuck in a rut. You live with the same problems, buried in the same lifestyle. The same mistakes roll over you, followed by the same poor decision-making process. The wheels of life roll over you and grind you into the ground.

Every day people are going up to the temple . . . and you are still in the same place.

Every day they go into the temple to pray . . . and you are still in the same place.

Every day they are passing you by . . . and you are still in the same place.

Every day their prayers are being answered . . . and you are still praying your same prayer.

You can see them go up and you can see them come down . . . but you are still in the same place.

People going in one way and coming out another . . . but you are still in the same place.

They are walking in and out, but you are sitting in the same place. You are close enough to see them go into the presence of God. You are close enough to look at them being blessed and being a blessing in worship. It is just an arm's length away, but you can't get in. You are still in the same place. Change never crossed your mind.

The man asked for alms, and Peter simply replied "We do not have what you want. We don't have what you are asking for; but we do have what you need." Sometimes, beloved, we need to remember that there is a difference between our wants and our needs. We want a lot of things, but we need only some things. We want a Mercedes, but need only a Chevrolet. We want a black diamond, but need only a fabulous fake. We want caviar, but fried chicken is what we need. Wants tend to satisfy a desire and needs tend to satisfy a necessity. Peter said, "We do have what you need; it is the name of Jesus." "In the name of Jesus Christ of Nazareth rise up and walk" (Acts 3:6).

The name of Jesus loosed the power of God to work in the man's body, strengthening his ankles and his feet. It was not the person of Jesus Christ, because he died, was buried and rose from the grave. Jesus was not there physically, but the healing took place because of the name of Jesus Christ. Ancients believed that the name of a person carried both the power and the authority of that person. Therefore, if a king sent a messenger in his name, that messenger represented the same power and the same authority as that king.

When the name of Jesus was spoken, or when someone speaks in the name of Jesus, the same power and authority of Jesus is now in his name. The same power over heaven and earth is now in his name.

The power to multiply.

The power to still the wind and the waves is in his name.

The power to forgive.

The power to heal and the power to deliver are in his name.

The power to raise the dead.

All hail the power of Jesus' name. At the name of Jesus, every knee shall bow and every tongue shall confess that Jesus Christ is Lord. There is no other name under heaven by which we can be saved. Both the power and the authority of Jesus are in the name of Jesus. When we have power, that means we have the strength, the influence, and the means to act. Power means the presence, ability and capability to do whatever needs to be done. Power is different from authority, however. Authority means that you may not have the influence, strength, means, capability or the ability to do what needs to be done. Authority is when you have been authorized to use the power outside of yourself, or the power of another source; you are authorized to handle their power. It is not your power, but the authorized power of another agent that is greater than your own. The authorized use of power gives you their capacity and capability to do whatever needs to be done.

In the name of Jesus is the Lord's power and authority. Jesus gave you permission to use his name. He said, "I don't want you to pray like you have been praying; this time when you pray, use my name." When you pray in the name of Jesus, the power and authority of Jesus is released in the prayer.

When Peter said "in the name of Jesus," it was the power and the authority of Jesus that loosed the power of God into the lame man's life. The name of Jesus, then, was a trigger to release the power. A trigger activates a mechanism that discharges power from a weapon. In order to get power from one place to another, you have to have an activation device. The trigger is the activation mechanism that precipitates a reaction. It sets up a chain reaction that initiates the power.

The name of Jesus is the trigger that initiates the power of God in the direction of the name. It activates the loosed guns of heaven, and power moves at the sound of the name. Heaven comes to attention when the name is spoken and dispatches power. Angels begin to move at God's command. Deliverance packs its bag and gets ready to move. Healing gets in a hurry and hope is encouraged, just because of the name of Jesus.

There is power when you preach in the name of Jesus.

There is power when you pray in the name of Jesus.

There is power when you witness in the name of Jesus.

There is power when you go in the name of Jesus.

There is power when you serve in the name of Jesus.

There is power when you touch in the name of Jesus.

There is power when you work in the name of Jesus.

There is power when you worship in the name of Jesus.

Many times we need more power to face the challenges of life and the enemies of God; only a spiritual Uzi will do.

When Peter spoke the name of Jesus to the lame man, understand that he had everything he needed to walk—but he could not walk. The lame man had everything he needed to walk: he had feet; he had ankles; he had legs; he had knees; he had hips; he had tendons; he had muscles. He had all of the basic equipment that God issues to every human being, yet he could not walk. He had everything he needed except the power of God working in his life. When the power in the name was released, the man was able to walk. The lame man looked at Peter and took his eyes off of himself. He looked away from his rut and looked up toward his help.

The Bible says that immediately the man got up and walked. Although the problem was long-term and severe, the cure was immediate. It was an instant change that did not occur because of a touch from Jesus or the laying on of hands. At the *name* of Jesus, "same" got out of the rut, got in touch with the good ground beneath, and changed. It leaped, and jumped, and praised God. What made the difference in the man's life was the power of God.

At the beginning of the text, the same man used to beg at the gate called Beautiful. At the end of the text, the power of God transformed his life. Some of us are like the lame man. Some of our churches and many of our ministries are like the lame man. We have everything we need to make it right. We have the intellect, the social standing, and the status. We have the equipment, structure, and success. We have skills and talent. We have attendees, givers, and members. We have everything we need to make it work, except we have no power. No power!

What we need is the power of God released into our lives.

What will happen to our churches if we do not speak the name of Jesus?

What will happen to our preaching if we utter the words of God in Jesus' name and the power of God is released?

What will happen to our singing if we sing in the name of Jesus—when the power of God is released in our anthems and in our hymns?

What will happen in our prayer lives, praying in his name?

What will happen in our marriages, our homes and families?

What will happen in our children's lives if we give them what they need, the released power of God, instead of what they want, Nikes, and the like? When we gather ourselves together, signs and wonders will follow the preached word of God.

What was missing from the lame man's life was the power of Jesus, and when the power of God was released in him, the text reveals that he went into the temple jumping and praising. It was a place that was formerly denied to him . . . a place that was out of reach. It was in view but it was out of reach, and when the power of God is activated in your life, you will go places that you have never gone and do things that you have never done.

The lame man's neighbors were amazed. They whispered, "Is this the same man?" Sometimes we live with the mistaken impression that things will always be the same.

When the power of God is released in your life, others will ask, "Is this the same man?"

"Is this the same woman?"

"Is that the same church that used to…?"

"Is this the same child that used to…?"

"…the same family that used to…?"

No, we are not the same anymore. Sometimes we live with the mistaken impression that things will always be the same. Nothing will ever be the same when the power of God is activated—Same No More!

NOTE

1. Zora Neale Hurston, *Their Eyes Were Watching God* (New York: HarperCollins, 1990). Originally published in 1937.

11
GIVING BIRTH

DIANE GIVENS MOFFETT

JOHN 16:19-21, KJV

Orator and freedom fighter Frederick Douglass, in one of his passionate speeches about the abolition of slavery said, "Where there is no struggle there is no progress."[1] Douglass was letting his listeners know that if they would give birth to the child of freedom, they would have to prepare themselves for hard labor. If they would move in the struggle for emancipation, they would have to prepare to give birth to liberation. It is no different for us today. Indeed it is true:

Where there are no guts, there is no glory.
Where there is no pain, there is no gain.
Where there is no battle, there is no blessing.

Birth comes after labor; fruit comes after planting; pleasure comes after perseverance. If we want to deliver the substance of our life and legacy—to bring forth that which developed in the womb of our consciousness—then it would behoove us to prepare for birth.

Wise mothers are depicted as—

Women who give and receive
Women who bear and share

Women who germinate and cultivate
Women who till and nurture
Women who sow and nurture—
Women who bring life and give life
Women who appreciate their gender and respect their femininity
Women who know the power and pleasure of having been
    created female—
Women who love being women!
The wise mother—prepares for birth.

For some mothers, morning sickness creeps up—queasiness, nausea, upset stomach, and lethargy set in. You begin to live to sleep and sleep to live. Your hormones send your emotions on a roller coaster ride. And not only do you go through emotional changes, you go through physical changes as well. All of the sudden, you find that you have an abundance of padding and curves in places that you did not have before. And that would be fine, but most of us already have enough padding on our frames! The pressure from the child you are carrying may cause your back to ache, your feet to swell, your body to sweat, and your mind to look forward to the day when the child shall appear. You look around and you notice that your hips are expanding and your chest is reaching out to new dimensions—a change, a change is coming over you. When you go to the doctor, she tells you, "It's all a part of the preparation for delivery—giving birth." Giving birth will take you through changes!
    And likewise, wise fathers are described as—

Men who plant and empower
Men who build and bless
Men who deposit and return
Men who caress and comfort
Men who create life and support life
Men who bring life and give life
Men who honor their gender and affirm their masculinity

Men who know the difference between making a baby and
   being a father—
I'm talking about real men!
The wise father—prepares for birth.

Men, too, go through changes in preparing for birth, wondering if you will make it through the actual delivery without falling out. Wondering how you will provide for the new addition in your life. Wondering what kind of father you will be. Wondering about your wondering. All of it is a part of the human experience of giving birth. Although men do not give birth in the physical sense, they do so in the spiritual sense. Yes, giving birth is a spiritual reality that both men and women experience. It is a reality that the disciples in our text are facing.

As Jesus approached his final hour, the time of crucifixion—the hour when he would lose his life so that you and I might find ours—he spoke to the disciples about giving birth. Jesus spoke of giving birth, not in the literal sense, but in the spiritual sense of being willing to go through the crucifixion in order to get to the resurrection in our lives. Using the analogy of a woman in labor, he let the disciples know that they were experiencing a spiritual birth. Like a caring and empathic midwife—Jesus began coaching the disciples, and us, regarding preparation for birth. He let us know that while the world may be rejoicing, moving on, oblivious to the pain that we suffer—God is in touch with our birthing process. God will be there to coach us through the delivery process—to wipe our feverish forehead when the fire of affliction heats up; to guide us through the preparation of delivery so that we will be able to stand when our hours come.

Some of us may need some coaching right now. Some of us may be going through the birth process right now. We are confused and frustrated, perplexed and dismayed, at a difficult point in our life. We are going up, as the old African American hymn says, "the rough side of the mountain." We may feel like throwing in the towel right now, but don't give up on your dream! Don't destroy the vision! Don't abort the baby! Don't end the pregnancy! Remind yourself of the words of Jesus, "When a woman is in labor, she has pain, because her hour has come. But when her child is born, she no longer remembers the anguish because of the joy of having brought a human being into the world" (John 16:21, NRSV).

Hold on until the delivery is complete!

Hold on until the situation changes!

Hold on until sorrow melts into joy and pain simmers into pleasure! Hold on!

Breathe through the contractions of life, concentrate and focus on that which God is birthing in you so that you may know the joy of God's promise. Wise disciples will not give up before time. Wise disciples learn how to prepare for giving birth; how to prepare for delivery so that when the labor pains come they will know how to handle them, and so they will be strong enough to ride the wave, move through the moment, and succeed in the situation. The statement begs the question, How then does one prepare for giving birth? Well, there are three basic instructions given to pregnant mothers. These same instructions can be used for pregnant disciples: eat well; exercise daily; and get plenty of rest.

EATING WELL

Doctors tell pregnant mothers to watch what they eat. Some pregnant women use the pregnancy as an excuse to go on a "see food" diet: when you see food, you eat it! But the doctors will tell you to eat those foods that will help you and your unborn child to be strong and healthy. The doctor will supply vitamins and minerals that will aid in keeping you strong and healthy. When a pregnant mother eats well and takes her vitamins, she better prepares herself for the delivery process.

Life is beating up on some of us and we are weak. We are weak because we have not been eating right. We have been on a see food diet, too. We see *Ebony, Jet, Essence,* and *EM, Black Enterprise,* and Oprah's magazines in the grocery store, on the newsstand, in the train stations, in the beauty salon, and the "washing house." We see them and we read them. We see the newspaper and we read it. We get that juicy novel and we read it. Well, there is nothing wrong with reading. We need to read to keep informed. The trouble comes when we fail to read the Word of God.

Consider the difference between a strong cup of tea and a weak one. The same ingredients—water and tea—are used for both. The difference is that the strong cup of tea results from longer immersion of the tea leaves in the water. The longer the steeping process, the stronger the cup of tea.

In the same way, the amount of time we spend reading God's Word determines how deeply we get into the Word, and the Word into us. Just like the tea, the longer we are in the Word, the "stronger" we become. In the Word we receive spiritual nutrients that will aid us in giving birth. We will need these nutrients when we are going through the birthing process. The nutrients from Scripture give us something to draw from when the hour comes and delivery gets rough. The Word helps to keep us strong when hard decisions need to be made. The Word will fortify us when the stuff hits the fan and the devil gets busy . . . for when the hour arrives, we become like a tea bag in hot water— what is in us comes out!

Rewind the biblical narrative and go down Mark's street, chapter one, verse nine. There you will find Jesus in "hot water." After forty days and forty nights, at Jesus' weakest point, the devil came to tempt him. But what was in the Son of Man came out! Each time the devil—with his slippery, slimy ways—came to challenge Jesus, Jesus spoke the Word back to him: "It is written. . . ."

When we are going through the birthing process, we have to learn to say, It is written. . . .

When the wait seems long and the vision seems to fade, we have to learn to say, It is written. . . .

When we are tired of the work and the race makes us weary, we have to learn to say, It is written. . . . "They who wait on the Lord shall renew their strength" (Isaiah 40:31). It is written, "The race is not to the swift, but to the person who endures till the end" (Ecclesiastes 9:11).

When the pain is deep and the sorrow high, we've got to learn to say, It is written, "Though weeping may endure for the night, joy comes in the morning" (Psalm 30:5).

When we are feeling forlorn and forsaken, we have to learn to say, It is written, "As a father pities a son, so I will pity you" (Psalm 103:13). As a mother comforts a child, I will comfort you. "And you shall be comforted" (Isaiah 66:13).

When we taste grief and sample bitter sorrow, we have to remember Jesus' words and learn to say, It is written, "You will have sorrow but your sorrow will turn into joy" (John 16:20).

If we want to arise in the power of the Spirit—if we want new life, we must learn to say, "It is written. . . ." Eat well and grow strong in the Word!

EXERCISING OUR FAITH

How do we prepare for giving birth? First of all eat well, and then exercise. Doctors tell pregnant women (and all of us for that matter) to get in shape by exercising. Exercise helps prepare our bones and limbs and muscles so that when the hour comes we will endure. In the same way, disciples in the delivery process have to exercise; but not so much the bones, and limbs, and muscles—we gave to exercise our faith. Exercising faith means trusting God enough to say, "Yes" in the midst of difficult labor; to say "Yes" in the crucifying moments; to say "Yes" when the waters of trouble wash over you; to say, "Yes" when the hour comes believing in the sure and certain hope of God's resurrection power.

So ladies, are you feeling rejected because, after fifteen years of marriage, he has left you with two kids and a mortgage? He said he needs to "find himself," which means: lose you and turn you in for a new 25-year-old model who has the body to impress, but not the brains or wisdom to know that the old sayings are sure and true:

"You shall reap what you sow."

"What goes around comes around."

"Everybody plays the fool sometime."

Wipe your eyes; your hour has come! Comb your hair; your hour has come. Put on your makeup; your hour has come. Decide to not only live, but to live abundantly! God is birthing something new in your life. Exercise your faith and say, It is written, "God will supply all my needs according to his riches in glory" (Philippians 4:19).

So you have lost a loved one. You feel empty and drained. Every day is a challenge and every night brings misery . . . do not fret. Thank God for the time you shared together and realize that this is a new day. Your hour has come! Exercise your faith knowing that God's plans for you are for good and not evil; to give you a garland instead of ashes; the oil of gladness instead of mourning; and a garment of praise instead of a spirit of despair that you will be called an oak of righteousness. Spread your branches and grow in the Spirit. Exercise faith and say, It is written, "The Lord is my light and my salvation . . ." (Psalm 27:1).

So you don't have the money now. You are broke and unemployed. You are not sure where your next paycheck is coming from. You have put out hundreds of resumes and still not been offered a job. Be not dismayed, your hour has come! Let your extremity become God's opportunity. Exercise faith. Say, It is written . . . "God can open doors that no one can shut, and shut doors that no one can open" (Revelation 3:8). Keep sending the resumes. Keep going to the interviews. Do not stop until you see the delivery process is over. Your hour has come!

So the church is going through some things. It seems that the vision is fading and that you will not ever get to your purpose. Officers and members have begun to play ecclesiastical politics and the membership is scattered. Be not dismayed, your hour has come! Exercise faith and say to yourself, It is written, "The gates of hell shall not prevail" against the church (Matthew 16:18). Keep working hard! Keep focused! Your hour has come! It is the time of decision. Exercise your faith; say "yes" to God and trust in God's Word.

GETTING PLENTY OF REST

How do we prepare for giving birth? By eating well, exercising our faith, and getting plenty of rest.

Giving birth will make you tired; ask any mother. Rest becomes a necessary part of your daily routine. Rest allows you to regain the strength and energy to move forward in the delivery process. In the same way, when God is birthing something in you—a new beginning, a new dream, a new season in your life—you will need rest. Not only do you need the sweet slumber of sleep, but the rest that comes when you pause for prayer—allowing spirit to speak to spirit, soul to speak to soul, and deep to call to deep. When you rest in the Lord, God renews you and strengthens you for delivery ahead.

When you are in the delivery process, the stress and strain mounts up on every side—at work and at home, in the community and in the church, in private and in public—folks just seem to pull on you and drain every ounce of energy from the cup of your life. If you are not careful to rest you will suffer from "drain out." But if you will take the time to get some rest, if you will rest in the Lord, God will pour into your soul God's marvelous power—pour until it saturates you; pour until it penetrates every part of your being; pour until your cup runs over with a strength and tenacity that comes only from the Spirit's power.

Our African American ancestors knew how to rest in the Lord. They knew how to pray to their Maker and connect with the Connector. Resting gave them the strength they needed to endure the atrocities of slavery and win your freedom and mine. Wise disciples followed the legacy of our African ancestors. Wise disciples, like the Reverend Dr. Martin Luther King Jr., know how to rest when delivery has become almost unbearable. In the process of giving birth to the civil rights movement that you and I must now work to protect and keep, Dr. King spoke in a sermon about how tired he was. He said that he kneeled down in prayer one evening, and the words to that old African American spiritual came to mind:

Sometimes I feel discouraged,
And think my work in vain.
But then the Holy Spirit,
Revives my soul again.
There is a balm in Gilead to make the wounded whole.
There is a balm in Gilead to heal the sin sick soul.[2]

After that moment, he said God spoke to him, telling him to stand up for justice and righteousness, knowing that God would be with him always, even until the end of the world! With a revived soul and a new determination, he rose up and stayed in the battle for America's soul.[3]

Resting in the Lord allows your soul to be revived. When you rest in the Lord, seeking the Lord and citing the Lord, then you are able to receive the manna from heaven, the nutrients from the Rock, the nourishment from a Midwife who knows how to birth that which is within you. No wonder Jesus says, "Come unto me, all ye that labour and are heavy laden, and I will give you rest" (Matthew 11:28). He is calling us today, to do as the songwriter suggests:

Rest in God—who is the lover of your soul.
Rest in God, who still has it all under control.
God is the Alpha and the Omega, the beginning and end.
God is your heavenly Parent. God will provide.
Rest in God, who desires to bless you everyday.
Rest in God, who hears you each time you pray.
All you've got to do is rest in God.[4]

Rest in the Lord so that when the hour comes you will have an internal anchor that will allow you to endure until the end!

When the hour came for Jesus, he gave it his all. When the hour came, Jesus said, "Yes." He endured the crucifixion, experienced the resurrection, and now sits at the right hand of God—praying for us, pleading with us, and reminding us that the birth is worth the labor. The crucifixion won't overshadow the resurrection! Keep pushing! Keep panting! Keep praying! Keep laboring. The joy of birth is coming. New life is on the way!

NOTES

1. Frederick Douglass, *My Bondage and My Freedom* (Miller, Orton, and Mulligan, 1855).
2. "Balm in Gilead." Negro spiritual in the public domain.
3. Martin Luther King Jr. in a sermon recorded on the album "In Search of Freedom" (Chicago: Mercury Records Corporation, 1970).
4. Paraphrase of the lyrics by Beverly Glenn, "Rest in Me." Lexicon Music, Inc. and Dixon Music, 1980.

12

HOW TO HANDLE A CRISIS BEFORE IT HANDLES YOU

ALFRED A. OWENS JR.

PSALM 57:1, KJV

The most spiritual person in the world faces crises—turning points of sudden, unpredictable, and unexpected occurrences. What makes something a crisis is the fact that we have no apparent control over the situation. I am talking about crises that we do not bring upon ourselves; for some of us are going through things that are the result of our own doing. Since we sowed bad seeds, now we must find a way to undo a bad harvest, or find a way to live through it. I am talking about times when we find ourselves faced with a situation in which we do not know how to proceed.

Things happen, even to the saints, even to the best of us, with all of our faith, all of our power from the Holy Spirit, and all of our shouting and praising God. Even with all of these things we cannot stop crises from coming into our lives.

We may as well admit it—things fall apart.

We may as well admit it—things come loose.

We may as well admit it—things break down, and crises come even in our spiritual lives.

That is why some who preach prosperity are no longer popular. God does want you to prosper in all areas, including finances, according to 3 John 2. Yet, the same Book that pronounces blessings on us also reveals, "In this world, you will have tribulation" (John 16:33).

We are going to have some hardships. We are going to have some trials and tribulations, and some crises are going to knock on our doors. A lot of people have quit the church, quit pastors, and some have even quit Jesus because they put their hope in preachers who said, "Let me lay my hands on you, and everything is going to be all right."

This is not biblical. We have to climb some mountains in our Christian walk; and sometimes, it is the rough side of the mountain that we must climb. Sometimes, it is a hard climb with no trolley car to take us to the top; and at other times, it is a hard slide back into the valley. Life is not all mountaintops or valleys, but a mixture.

We are not going to be crisis-free.

We are not going to be burden-free.

We are not going to be trial-free.

We have to do more than cry our way through life. We need to know how to handle a crisis situation without panicking and making things worse. The Lord gave me a "911" Scripture—a way to handle a crisis situation, a way to get hold of him at a time when things are crucial, critical, and unstable. I found the key in Psalm 57.

The context of Psalm 57 is found in 1 Samuel 22, a time when David was hiding in a cave from his jealous adversary, King Saul. Does that sound like a crisis to you? David was a fugitive from the king. To make matters worse, he was joined by other men who were also experiencing crises in their own lives. So crisis met crisis!

Have you ever felt like a fugitive? Have you ever felt as if you were in a cave, or felt like finding a cave? I am positive that every person has been in one, if not all three, of the dilemmas mentioned in the context of that event in David's life.

Saul was insanely jealous because he knew that David had been anointed to replace him as king. David escaped to the cave Adullam. When his brothers and those of his father's house heard where he was, they went to the cave, along with a number of other men. The Bible says that everyone who joined David was in debt and "bitter of soul" (1 Samuel 2:22), meaning discontented. Have you ever been down in the dumps, having problems yourself, only to have someone come and dump theirs on top of yours? Being the saint that you are, you cannot tell them to leave you alone.

Out of the four hundred men who eventually joined David, not one brought comfort. Yet this crisis formula, this "911" solution that I am going to show you, came out of this situation. God has shown me that the same thing will work today. In fact, when I first saw this in Psalm 57 and 1 Samuel, the Lord revealed to me that those men who joined David were in such bad shape that they were on the verge of a nervous breakdown, or even worse, suicide. However, because they looked to David for help, he had to come up with a solution. What he found is right there in Psalm 57:1: "Be merciful unto me, O God, be merciful unto me: for my soul trusteth in thee: yea, in the shadow of thy wings will I make my refuge, until these calamities be overpast."

Our "911" call letters are K-R-K-P. The first call letter in our solution is K; that stands for *know*. Psalm 57 says "the crisis came to pass." That means the three Ds came *to pass*.

Your Discontent came *to pass*.

Your inDebtedness came *to pass*.

Your Distress came *to pass*.

In other words, it did not come to last. When the pastor is not around, when the deacons, missionaries, and other saints are not around, there are certain things you have to know to get through a crisis. First, you have to know it is going to pass; it is not going to last. It came only to pass. Trouble does not last forever if you are a child of God. It does come to an end!

In the first verse of Psalm 57—a contemplation of David when he fled from Saul in the cave—David said he would take refuge "in the shadow" of God's wings "until these calamities be overpast." Overpast means passed over, or done with.

Have mercy on me, God, until these calamities have passed over me.

Cover me until these calamities have passed over me.

Stand by me until these calamities have passed over me.

The storm is passing over you, and you have to know that God did not bring you this far to leave you. This, too, shall pass. That is the first call letter of my signal for help in crisis.

Psalm 57:2 expresses the heart of our second call letter—R, for *remember*: "I will cry unto God most high; unto God that performeth all things for me." Remember the Source of all your help. I will cry, I will call, I will pray unto God most high. I will call on God, who has brought me out of other crises, because I have been 3D'ed before.

David said, "Not only am I going to know that this came to pass, but I am going to remember the Source of all my help in previous crises." The first thing the adversary wants you to do when you get into trouble is to forget what God has done already. The reason you panic and end up doing ridiculous things that worsen the situation is because you do not want to remember who was your help in times past.

David said, "I am going to remember when I was tending sheep, and the bear and the lion came. That was a crisis, but the Lord gave me victory. I am going to remember when Goliath would have killed me, but the Lord fought my battle. I am going to remember when I did not see how I was going to escape from Saul before, but God brought me out."

You must remember the *Source* of all your help. Your help does not come from 900 numbers. Your help does not come from the psychic connection. Your help does not come from lottery tickets, but your help comes from the Lord. David said that some trusted in horses, and some trusted in the sword, but he would trust in the Lord. He would call on God, who performed all things for him. God himself is the source of relief from distress, from debt, from discontentment. Look at verse 3 to see what David *knew* God would do:

He shall send from heaven, and save me from the reproach
of him that would swallow me up. Selah. God shall send
forth his mercy and his truth.

In verses 4 and 6, he outlined his crisis situation:

My soul is among lions: and I lie even among them that are
set on fire, even the sons of men, whose teeth are spears and
arrows, and their tongue a sharp sword. . . . They have prepared a net for my steps; my soul is bowed down: they have
digged a pit before me, into the midst whereof they are fall-
en themselves. Selah.

Not only was Saul after him, but four hundred men whose souls
were "set on fire," whose teeth were "spears and arrows," and
whose tongues were like "sharp swords" were following him, too.
Have you ever had someone come against you whose tongue
seemed sharp as a sword?

David admitted that he was discouraged. His soul was "bowed
down" because his enemies—Saul and company—had prepared
a net for his feet and dug a pit for him. However, in the midst of
that pit, guess what happened? They fell into it themselves. Has
anyone ever set a trap for you? Have folks ever dug a ditch or a
pit, expecting you to fall into it, and then fell into it themselves?

Like David, you must remember that when God is on your
side, people can dig ditches and set traps, but "no weapon
formed against you will prosper" (Isaiah 54:17). People may
dig a pit, but it will not prosper. Do not let the devil know all
your secrets—God is in control. You have to know that money
did not get you this far, education did not get you this far,
and good looks did not get you this far in life. Your help comes
from the Lord.

The second K of our call letters is gleaned from verse 7:
"My heart is fixed, O God, my heart is fixed; I will sing and
give praise." That sounds as if David had to remind himself,
just as we sometimes have to remind ourselves. He repeated,
"My heart is fixed," as a reminder. Our second K is *keep*. We

must keep our hearts fixed on God. In a crisis, the devil comes to mess with our hearts and to put our emotions in chaos.

My eyes may be dim, but my heart is fixed.

My ears may be dull, but my heart is fixed.

My knees may be shaking, but my heart is fixed.

My hands may be weak, but my heart is fixed.

The devil wants to move the condition of our hearts, but while we are going through crises, we must keep our hearts rooted and grounded in God. We cannot let it sway to the right or to the left.

What happens to many of us when our finances move? Our heart moves. We are as happy as we can be when we have money; we are as agreeable, loving, and as nice as we can be. However, when our money moves, our heart moves. Yet David says it does not matter about this temporary condition in the cave, this momentary distress, this temporary indebtedness, because my heart is fixed. I cannot speak for another, but

I am not going to develop heart trouble over debt.

I am not going to get heart trouble over distress.

I am not going to get heart trouble over discontentment.

Jesus said for us to not let our hearts be troubled (John 14:1). That means that he is our heart-fixer as well as our heart-keeper. Let everything around us shake and move, but we must keep our hearts in one place. Why is it so important that we keep our hearts fixed? The answer is found in the last of our call letters—P.

David was a musician, and in that cave around all those distressed, debt-ridden, discontented folks, he had let his heart be cast down. The devil will make you put down what God has given you. David said in verse 8, "I know you gave me this harp and the ability to sing, God. I know you taught me how to play. Awake, psaltery and harp! My heart is fixed."

I do not care what else moves, do not let that movement affect your heart. It may affect your pocketbook, but not your heart. It may affect your transportation, but not your heart. Keep your heart fixed on God.

The last of our four letters is found in Psalm 57:9-11: "I will praise thee, O Lord, among the people: I will sing unto thee among the nations. For thy mercy is great unto the heavens, and thy truth unto the clouds. Be thou exalted, O God, above the heavens: let thy glory be above all the earth."

Praise God, that is your P. Praise God in the midst of a crisis, and that is hard to do. If you believe that God is in the midst of everything, when do you have to praise him? You cannot wait until you get out of a crisis to praise him. David did not wait until he got out of that cave. David said, "Wake up here, give me my psaltery, and give me my harp. All of you distressed, in-debt, discontented men, get up here, and praise God in the midst of it. Praise God among the people."

When I *know* that any crisis is going to pass, and when I *remember* my Source, and *keep* my heart fixed on him, I am going to *praise* him in the midst of troubles and trials. If you are in your cave of Adullam, and friends think they ought to come into your cave to mourn with you, surprise them. Shout, "Give me my harp, and give me my psaltery! I have been in this pity party too long. If God wants Saul to have me, so be it. If God wants my enemy to swallow me up, so be it. But the God I serve is not like that. God told me a long time ago, before I got in this cave, that he is my light and my salvation. The Lord is the strength of my life; of whom shall I be afraid?"' (Psalm 27:1).

If you keep on looking in the midst of the three Ds, in the midst of distress, in the midst of debt, in the midst of discontentment, there is another D, called Deliverance. God sent deliverance to the cave. David and those distressed, indebted, discontented men came out with the victory. Don't stop until you reach the deliverance!

God said that each of us, like David, can be delivered from the caves of life. God showed David what to do when people did not like him, and the Lord will show us the same thing today just as quickly. However, we must be like David and look to God as our only Source for help, strength, and wisdom.

13

THE BURDEN AND BLESSING OF BLACKNESS

JAMES C. PERKINS

MARK 15:21, KJV

Throughout the broad scope of human existence, no race or nation has been subjected to such cruel and systematic suffering as have we, the people whose skin has been made black by nature's sun. For some strange and unknown reason, the color of our skin has caused us to be looked upon as inferior in the eyes of the world, and treated like brute beasts, chattel property, and everything else except children of God. All sorts of explanations have been ventured in an attempt to shed some light on the reason of our wretched plight. But no explanation can justify the unspeakable atrocities that have been inflicted upon us since the veritable beginning of time.

Some have tried to use the Bible to imply that God has condemned us to be the slaves of the human race. But if the Bible is not clear about anything else, it is explicit about the fact that God made of one blood all nations of persons to dwell upon the face of the earth (Acts 17:26). God is the omnipotent Creator and the benevolent parent of us all. To imply that God destined and ordained us to be treated as we have been is a lie that only the devil could conceive, and that demon spirits could promote. But as tragic as it is, this is the untruth that has been perpetuated about black people since the beginning of recorded history.

In all the literature stretching back into the dusty volumes of antiquity, black people have been referred to in negative and demeaning ways. Now and then we hear about the singular contributions of black individuals, but never is there any mention of our positive contributions as a race. Collectively, we are almost always referred to in negative ways. We have been written out of history, and we have been included only when it is convenient to portray us as slaves or crooks.

This is why it is so important for us to discover, to learn, and to research our history. When we do not know who we are, where we have been, or how we got where we are, others will write our history for us. But they will not mention the contributions we have made to the welfare of the world. They will not present us fairly, as we are, but rather as they perceive us; as they want others to perceive us; as they want us to perceive ourselves.

No explanation has emerged that clears up the mystery of the pitiful plight of we who Franz Fanon has called "the wretched of the earth." Our history is a paradox. On the one hand, we get rumors about our having been, at some point in time, a highly accomplished and civilized race. Within a limited circle, we are praised as being the first in almost every sphere of human endeavor. We hear about the glory that once belonged to Egypt. We hear rumors that Ethiopia shall stretch forth her arms again. But on the other hand, we are accused of being cursed by God; we have been blamed for the deterioration and decay of every society and civilization where we have lived.

There appears to be a conspiracy to cover up or to destroy our history in an effort to keep us from learning about ourselves. Perhaps the world knows that if we ever discover, by research and conviction, that we are not innately inferior, and that God ordained us for some special purpose, they will not be able to constrain and oppress us, nor to intimidate, denigrate, or to destroy us.

Be that as it may, history does seem to have assigned us to the basement of the human family. Why? We simply do not know.

Why black people have suffered as a group, or why anybody suffers for that matter, remains a mystery. And so it must be until that bright clear morning in the "sweet by and by" when the mist is rolled away, when the clouds are lifted, and when the meaning of human experience is seen in its stark nakedness. Then all questions will be answered. Then all mysteries will be dispelled. Then all revelations will be unraveled. Then all secrets will be made known. What we do not understand about our trying experience now is why, as one low-spirited brother put it, "we have to be so black and blue." If we keep faith in God and in life, if we keep on serving God though the burden gets heavy and the teardrops fall, we will understand it better by and by. For in that morning bright and fair, the God who made us black also will make the mystery plain.

The many centuries of inhumane treatment have deposited in our collective psyche some deep and painful scars. Through it all, however, the worst thing that has happened to us is that we have been programmed to hate ourselves. Living in a world that seems bent on our destruction, surviving in an environment of contempt and hatred, and centuries of programming to think of ourselves as less than human—all of these forces have taken their toll. Nobody could live through such vicious hostility and emerge unscarred and unscathed.

All of these negative experiences have caused us to feel ashamed of ourselves, just because of an act of nature. We have harbored hatred for the way that God had made us. We have sung songs and prayed prayers like "Lord, wash me whiter than snow." We have chemically processed our naturally curly hair to try to make it stringy and straight. We have bleached our skin to lighten our natural color. We have played favoritism toward the "yellow blacks" and we resented the "blue blacks."

No other group of people has suffered through an identity crisis like ours. First we were colored. Then we were Negroes. Then we were black. Later we were Afro-Americans. Now we are African Americans. But when we called ourselves black, it represented a significant spiritual victory in our march toward fulfillment. It represented the victory of self-definition. Others had defined us as being colored or Negro, but "black" is the name we chose to call ourselves. We had struggled with our blackness, and we had rejected our blackness. Many of us are old enough to remember a time when, if you called another person black, you had to fight.

But by the grace of God, we came to accept ourselves. We refused to allow others to define us and we became both black and proud. This was, I say, a significant spiritual victory; for the first step in going anywhere is knowing who you are. People cannot intimidate you when you know who you are. The names people call you do not offend you when you know who you are. There are certain things to which you simply will not stoop when you know who you are.

People look at the weak and the lost elements among us and conclude that all of us are lazy and shiftless; that we have no or low aim. They dismiss us as a blotch of worthless humanity. They forget that these responses, in large measure, are the ugly residue left by centuries of being enslaved, segregated, Jim-Crowed, ostracized, despised, ghettoized, and criticized. With all we have suffered, it is a miracle that black people have survived at all.

Black people have suffered to such an awful extent that blackness no longer refers to simply the color of our skin. Blackness has come now to represent the suffering condition of all oppressed people everywhere. Looking at it in this context, to be black means to suffer. To be black means to be oppressed. To be black means to be numbered among the disenfranchised and the disinherited.

It may sound like strange music tap dancing on the tympanic membrane of our inner ear, but when we talk about blackness in a symbolic sense, it is perfectly proper to say that Jesus had a black experience.

Jesus was despised and rejected.

Jesus did not help the big fish swallow up the little fish.

Jesus did not side with the power structure. He was committed to transforming it.

Jesus' preaching got him into trouble with the government. One of his disciples even became a government informant and turned him over to the authorities.

Jesus was arrested without being told the nature of the charges levied against him, what law he had broken, or what crime he had committed.

Jesus was tried without a lawyer or a jury.

In fact, Jesus was found guilty even before he was arrested.

They tried him at night when no official court was in session.

They tried him five times in four courts and he didn't get justice in any of them.

They released a known criminal who had been found guilty in a trial by jury just so they would have a cross available on which to hang Jesus.

Like Rodney King, Jesus was a victim of police brutality. For the word is that they whipped him all night long.

When we recognize what an awful miscarriage of justice Jesus experienced, we can identify this as a black experience. For we as black people—we as suffering people, we as oppressed people—we know something about the miscarriage of justice. The justice of this world seems to work for anybody who has enough money to buy it. In fact, it seems to work for everybody except—just us.

There is another instance of the miscarriage of justice being reported to us in this text. It too involves a black man whose name is unknown to many of us. As the Roman soldiers led Jesus toward the place of execution on crucifixion morning, Jesus was so weak and exhausted from the brutality of the night before that he fell beneath the weight of his cross. The soldiers kicked him, lashed him, and demanded that he get up and keep the ill-fated procession moving towards Calvary. But Jesus was physically too weak to go any farther.

The soldiers looked around and there happened to be a black

man named Simon from Cyrene, a city that was located in mod-ern-day Libya. Him they compelled to carry the cross for Jesus. Simon just happened to be passing by, and they compelled him to carry the cross. And this is the burden of blackness. We have not done anything to deserve the horrible treatment we have experienced. Like Simon, we just happened to be there. We are victims of circumstance.

Our color has been a burden for us. It has caused us to be denied opportunities we may have had. It has caused us to be ridiculed for no good reason. It has caused us to be humiliated without provocation. We constantly have to prove ourselves; and even when we are better than the best, still it is not good enough. We have built societies and economies that we cannot enjoy. That is the burden of blackness. That means that we have been forced to do everything on earth there is to be done, including help Jesus bear the cross!

Sure, Jesus—a Jew by nationality; Son of God by creation; Savior of the world by consent—sure, Jesus hung on the cross, but a black man carried that cross to Calvary.

Simon, a Cyrenian passerby, a black man who had his own agenda mapped out for the day, had to scrap his plans because they compelled him. They did not ask him. In fact, nobody has asked politely for a black man to do anything. They compelled him. They forced him. They compelled him to carry Jesus' cross.

Simon shrank from this awful ordeal. "Sirs, I'm in a hurry. My family is expecting me shortly."

But the insensitive soldiers insisted, "Come here, boy."

Simon replied, "But, sirs, it's a cross. It's not fair. I'm trying to set a proper example for my two sons. You know a cross carries with it a terrible stigma. I don't want to make them ashamed. I want to make them proud. And how can I if word gets about that I've borne a cross?"

"Bend your back, boy."

"And they compel one Simon, a Cyrenian who passed by coming out of the country, the father of Alexander and Rufus, to bear his cross."

Simon, a black man, took upon his strong, sturdy, steady, stable black shoulders the old rugged cross. The cross—representing the sins of the world. The cross—the emblem of suffering and shame. The cross—the instrument of the world's salvation.

Simon took upon his shoulders the old rugged cross. And therein lies the blessing of blackness. For in bearing that cross behind Jesus, Simon, a black man, helped the man who saved the whole world.

We have got a stake in this salvation business, because we helped Jesus to carry his cross. Our destiny as a people is tied up with Jesus and the cross. If we leave Jesus and the cross, we can forget our destiny.

Yes, it is a burden to be black. But the story of Simon teaches us that we can transform a burden into a blessing. We are not to use our blackness as an excuse. We are to bear our burden well; we are to bear it with such grit and grace; we are to bear it with such pride and perseverance; we are to bear it with such dignity and determination that, like Simon, we transform our burden into a blessing. This is what Jesus did by hanging on the cross. This is what Simon did by helping him to bear that cross.

The first lesson here is that we must learn how to . . .

TURN A NEGATIVE SITUATION INTO A POSITIVE EXPERIENCE

Simon might have allowed himself to be devastated by the situation he encountered on Good Friday morning. The cross carried with it a terrible stigma. He did not know Jesus from Adam. For all Simon knew, he was just carrying the cross of a condemned criminal. And on top of it all, he was forced to carry it against his will. Simon might have allowed this entire negative ordeal to embitter his spirit and anger him for the rest of his life. There are a whole lot of black people who are angry and bitter because of our circumstances in the world. They are mad with white people. They are mad with the power structure. They are mad with God. They are mad with life. They are just mad! They have allowed our negative situation to embitter them to the point that they have copped out of life and decided to be nothing and to do nothing.

But, my brothers and sisters, it does not matter what happens to us in this life, we must never allow any situation to affect us to the point that it makes us destroy ourselves. We have got to find a way to turn every negative situation into a positive experience.

I have no idea what Jesus said to Simon. I do not know what Simon saw in Jesus. But something happened in the process of bearing and sharing that cross that made Simon have a change of mind. Jesus makes the difference. Jesus can make something happen to you on the inside that changes the way you see things on the outside. Jesus on the inside works on the outside.

In the places where black people have Jesus, they are having church. They are serving the Lord, and trying to make something positive of their lives. In environments where blacks do not have Jesus, they are throwing themselves to the dogs.

There are a whole lot of people out there who are entangled and overcome by the deadly, negative, nasty situations around us rather than seeking a positive way out of the situation. A whole lot of us are trying to make blackness mean coolness. Listen, you may look good being hip, and slick, and cool, but you cannot survive simply by being cool. There are no jobs or job descriptions for cool folks. And now there is no welfare for them, either.

We have got to make blackness mean competent, not cool. We must make blackness mean qualified, dignified, saved, and sanctified.

It is not about whether the curls are laying right on your head. It is about whether you have something in your head. It is not about having expensive clothes on your back. It is about whether you have anything in your heart. It is not about whether you can rap. It is about whether you can read.

We cannot allow negative situations to overcome us. We have got to turn every negative situation into a positive experience.

That is what Jesus did by hanging from the cross. And that is what Simon did by helping him bear the cross.

WE MUST PASS ON A PROUD HERITAGE

This text points out that Simon was the father of Alexander and Rufus. Simon was so proud of helping Jesus bear his cross that he went on home and reared his two sons to be Christians, and they became prominent members of the early Christian church.

They were so prominent that when Mark sat down to write the Gospel and wanted everybody to know the Simon to which he was referring, he said, "Simon. . . . you know, Simon. The black fella' . . . Alexander and Rufus' daddy."

The sons were so prominent that Paul called Rufus' mother his mother (Acts 16:13). Somewhere in that old Roman Empire, Paul had met up with a black family and named a black woman as one of his mothers in the faith.

Simon passed on a proud heritage; and we do owe something to the generations that come after us, just like we do the generations that have come before us. We cannot live so shamefully that every time a black child is born into the world, they have another strike against them.

Our mothers and fathers passed on a wonderful heritage to us. We came from people who believed they could succeed against the odds . . .

We came from a long line of freedom fighters.

We came from people who knew how to take nothing and make something out of it.

We came from people who put their lives on the line for justice and equality.

We came from people who helped Jesus bear the cross that saved the world. We have a proud heritage, and we owe it to our forebears to pass that heritage on to the next generation.

Imagine how Simon must have felt later that Friday evening and all weekend long about having to carry that cross. He was so ashamed and humiliated that he could not go home right away. He decided to check himself into a little cheap motel on the outskirts of Jerusalem. He bought a half-gallon of that cheap Passover wine and spent the weekend getting drunk.

But imagine how he must have felt on Sunday morning when he awakened from his drunken stupor, and the headlines of his complimentary copy of the *Jerusalem Times* read, "Man Hanged on Center Cross Resurrected as Savior of the World."

Old Simon was not ashamed any more. He went running through the streets half naked shouting to everybody, "I was the man! I was the man who helped him! I helped him bear the cross!" My brothers and sisters, we have got to make blackness mean something in our time, something that you can be proud of rather than ashamed.

We have to start bearing the cross.

A proud heritage awaits you at the cross.

A sense of self and a sense of purpose are waiting for you at the cross.

A sense of dignity and self-esteem are yours for the claiming at the cross.

Bearing the cross requires discipline. It requires commitment of your life. This is your day. This is your opportunity. This is your responsibility to previous and future generations.

I see Jesus. I see him weak, bleeding, exhausted, and sore. I see him when he fell beneath the weight of his cross. And an angel was marching through the corridor of heaven bearing a silver tray to the throne. When that angel saw Jesus dropped beneath the weight of his cross, he could take it no more. The angel dropped his tray, ran to the edge of the universe, and shouted to all humankind, "Must Jesus bear the cross alone, and all the world go free?"[1]

And old, black Simon bowed his body, bent his back, and said, "No, for there is a cross for everyone; and there is a cross for me."

WE MUST SUFFER FOR SOMETHING WORTHWHILE

To be black is to suffer. Our color imposes and exposes us to a certain amount of suffering. We suffer by being regarded as inferior. We suffer by being ignored when jobs are available. There is some suffering we endure just because we are black. But there is some suffering that we do not have to endure. We do not have to suffer from ignorance. We can go to school. We do not have to suffer from the lack of jobs. We can be inventive and create our own jobs.

There is suffering that we endure simply because we are black. But there is some suffering we experience by choice. And since we have a choice, we ought to choose to suffer for something worthwhile. We can suffer to make the world a better place . . . suffer to make black mean beautiful. Suffer to build the kingdom of God on earth as it is in heaven. That is what it means to bear a cross. It means to suffer for the redemption of a person, a people, or a situation.

Rest assured that God takes note of that kind of suffering. At the end of cross bearing comes crown wearing.

No cross. No crown.

No contest. No conquest.

No battle fought. No victory won.

No pain endured. No peace enjoyed.

I am now like Simon, so I'm going to cherish that old rugged cross. I'm going to cling to it until I lay down my earthly trophies in exchange for that heavenly crown.

I am black, but I want my crown. And when the battle is over, we shall wear a crown in the New Jerusalem.

NOTES

1. "Must Jesus Bear the Cross Alone?" lyrics by Thomas Shepherd. Public domain.

14

THE DANGER OF AN UNGUARDED MOMENT

DENNIS V. PROCTOR

JOHN 13:27, KJV

ave you ever been shocked or surprised at the speech, behavior, or appearance of someone who professes to be a believer in God, or a follower of the Way? And has the discovery of an ethical lapse or moral failure in someone caused you to query, "How could they do that?" Has an injurious character flaw caused you to doubt the validity and sincerity of another person's walk or witness? Probably.

But before we venture too far down the path of people persecution, perhaps there should be another entry into our judgment journal. When was the last time you stunned yourself with a lack of spiritual stability? Have you been cut off in traffic lately, routed in an insufferably long line, spilled something on an expensive outfit, scuffed the toe on a new pair of shoes, missed the bus, or stayed in a heated verbal exchange one sentence too long, and out of nowhere, a stream of expletives—profanity—spewed forth from your mouth, or rushed through your mind with the force of Niagara Falls? If you have ever had to apologize for saying the wrong thing, feeling the wrong thing, or doing the wrong thing at the wrong time or in the wrong way to the wrong person, then you are familiar with the danger of an unguarded moment. If you have fondled a fleeting flirtation, dabbled with dishonesty, or abandoned your normal appetite of personal restraint and righteousness, then you are acquainted with what it means to have an unguarded moment.

Have you ever just cast off sense and sensibilities in order to join the prodigal son for a moment of "riotous living"? It is well documented that certain external stimuli can impact and imperil our pilgrimage toward perfection, so much so that a melody, a fragrance, a picture, or a remembrance can send us meandering off the straight and narrow path, and thrust us back down memory lane.

Even the most saintly have their moments, when their heavenly halos have been traumatized and tarnished by temptation. Since the inception of recorded time, episodes of regret and remorse have filled life's pages with personal improprieties.

- Adam, the apple of God's creation, was subject to an unguarded moment in the Garden of Eden. (Genesis 3:6)

- Abraham, the father of the faithful, experienced his fall in the face of Pharaoh. (Genesis 12:11-20)

- Esau, the son of privilege, had his moment when he sold his birthright in response to a physical craving. (Genesis 25:30-34)

- Moses, the servant of God, "lost it" one day in the wilderness, and as Bishop Clinton R. Coleman argued, lost the Promised Land when he smote the rock and made the people think that he was responsible for the water. (Numbers 20:9-12)

- Achan, the lowly foot soldier, had an unguarded moment when he hid the accursed thing under his tent. (Joshua 7:21)

- David, the man after God's own heart, had one of several moments, when he relished a rooftop romance, thus rupturing his relationship with the Lord. (2 Samuel 11:2-4)

- Peter, attempting to disassociate with the Lord and his program, began to curse and swear to prove

that he was not affiliated with that Jesus movement.
(Mark 14:70-71)

Bishop Alfred G. Dunston went so far as to sermonically suggest
that the entire nation of Israel had an unguarded moment as they
began whining in the wilderness (Exodus 17:2-3), hence "spoil-
ing one of life's finest moments."

This text points to one of the most trying and true tests of the
would-be follower of Christ. "And after the sop, Satan entered
into him." Our task is not to debate the existence, the nonexis-
tence, or the preexistence of Satan, the devil, el diablo,
Beelzebub, or demons. Suffice it to say that something unusual,
unholy, and unprofitable took hold of Judas. In a moment, in the
twinkling of an eye, he went from being full of the Spirit to being
full of the devil.

Further examination of this text shows some striking similari-
ties to the conflict of conscience and conduct often evident in
today's Christians. What at once arrests our attention are the
candidates who are capable of such contemptible character.

THE LEAST LIKELY PERSON

Judas should have been the least likely person capable of this
deed. Who would have ever pictured Judas Iscariot, the one
whose name means "Praise of God," doing such a thing? Judas,
the one who was physically close to the Lord, leaning on the
Lord, loved by the Lord, and as verse 29 shares, was lifted by the
Lord to a place of prominence in this fledgling congregation.
Judas, who was happy to keep the bag, dispense the money, and
monitor the budget. Judas, elevated from the obscurity of antiquity to the heights of notoriety! Judas, who was both called and
chosen. Judas, a founding member of the faithful few! How could
this happen to Judas—a card-carrying member of the ecclesiastical elite? Can't you see him comfortable in the King's presence,
being fed by his hand and favored by his love? What a scene of
tenderness—Jesus taking the bread and using it as a sponge, rem-
iniscent of those today who use biscuits, cornbread, or sliced
bread to "sop-up" the sauce, the gravy, bits of meat, or broth from

the plate. Judas was licking the Lord's fingers and yet, after the sop, Satan entered into him. He was the last person one would have expected or suspected to be a co-conspirator with Satan. However, a closer look at Judas shows telltale signs of an integrity slow leak and a fidelity failure.

In John 12:5-6, it was Judas who protested the display of affection showered on Jesus by a mournful Mary, saying, "'Why was not his ointment sold for three hundred pence, and given to the poor?' This he said, not that he cared for the poor; but because he was a thief, and had the bag, and bare what was put therein."

Tragically, Judas had been "dipping from the till," as it were, up to this point. Acts 1:18, 19 informs us, "Now this man purchased a field with the reward of iniquity . . . insomuch as that field is called in their proper tongue, Aceldama, that is to say, The field of blood."

It was a logical progression to move from thievery to treachery. Senior sages of our tradition used to caution against "winking at sin." They believed, "If you lie, you'll steal; and if you'll steal, you'll kill!" Perhaps they understood that what satisfies Satan today is inadequate to repeat the thrill on tomorrow. If unguarded moments go unchecked, unchallenged, and unconfessed, then what was a deviation from the divine design today becomes the rule, instead of the exception, tomorrow. Thirty pieces of silver proved to be a hefty inducement for one who valued the things of life over the Lord of life (see Matthew 26:14-16).

Lest we become too focused on the frailties of Judas, let us remember that every believer, like Judas, holds a special place in the mind of the Master, "[We] are a chosen generation, a royal priesthood, a holy nation, a peculiar people" (1 Peter 2:9).

Each time we give in to an unguarded moment, an alarm should go off in our spirits and say, "After all that the Lord has done for me, and with me, how can I allow Satan entrée into my space?" You are the least likely person to let the Lord down. After all, as more than one songwriter has said, just think of his goodness to you!

THE WORST POSSIBLE PLACE

Not only was Judas the least likely person, but his action occurred at the worst possible place. He was in the fellowship of the believers, communion of the saints. Miles Jones calls it "an enclave of intimacy." He was at the setting of the Last Supper, the Lord's Supper, and this was the prototype of the church. It ought to be abundantly clear that unguarded moments are no respecter of persons or places!

Do you believe that evil can intrude into the most sacred of places? Not even the upper room was off limits for satanic seduction. Why would it be? In the poetic Book of Job, the account reads, "Now there was a day when the [children] of God came to present themselves before the Lord, and Satan came also . . ." (Job 1:6).

It seems to reason that if this unsettling and unscrupulous presence can invade the celestial city, surely our churches, our homes, and our places of employment are equally accessible to the enemy. The Scripture says in verse 26 that Jesus was aware that there was contention and contamination in his congregation. Notwithstanding, the Lord did not point him out, pick him out, kick him out, fuss him out, or "cuss" him out. Judas must represent the aggregation in every congregation that I refer to as, "sinful, but necessary." Some people, problems, and pressures are necessary to keep us on our knees. Christian character is developed in the crucible, not the spiritual cradle. Our knees are still the best position to "Lift up [our] eyes unto the hills, from whence cometh [our] help. [Our] help cometh from the Lord" (Psalm 121:1-2).

Jesus just held his peace. How can the Lord ever prepare a table for us in the presence of our enemies if we disperse, dispatch, and dispense them as soon as they are discovered? A. Louis Paterson argues that when spirits congregate in your place of peace, the commotion they create merely represents the "hammer and nails of God constructing the table before you."

So, do not be alarmed when even among the "saved, sanctified, and spirit-filled crowd," you get a glimpse at less than the

glory of God. After all, the church is not a resort for the righteous, but a way station for the wounded, and a filling station for
the weary.

> Come ye disconsolate, where're ye languish,
> Come to the mercy seat, fervently kneel;
> Here bring your wounded hearts, here tell your anguish:
> Earth has no sorrow that heav'n cannot heal.[1]

Revelations of indiscretions in the church house, the White
House, the courthouse, schoolhouse, statehouse, or jailhouse
should give rise to the awareness that no place is sacrosanct. No
place is beyond the possibility of periodic personal impoverish-
ment. Unguarded moments are endemic and pandemic. They
are everywhere and wherever! Peter, who was no stranger to such
slip-ups or let downs, admonishes other sojourners, "Be sober, be
vigilant; because your adversary the devil, as a roaring lion,
walketh about, seeking whom he may devour" (1 Peter 5:8).

There was a seasoned saint who left home and family for an
opportunity to dwell with God in the wilderness. He enjoyed his
secluded, special time with the Lord. Unfortunately, he was constantly under attack by the forces of evil; yet they were never
able to seduce him with thoughts of money, power, sex, or pride.
Then one day, an aged demon said to his underlings, "You have
been using the wrong tactics! Go whisper in his ear that his
slothful brother has just been named Man of the Year!" Upon
hearing the news, an envious scowl came over his face, and his
spirit was defiled and disturbed. The demons had succeeded. He
resented the recognition given to his rebellious sibling. You can
worship in the wilderness, praise on the pinnacle, and shout in
the sanctuary, and still have an unguarded moment.

THE WORST POSSIBLE TIME
The most chilling dimension of this narrative is found in the first
clause of verse 27, "and after the sop."

It is unfathomable that immediately after communion with

Christ, Satan could enter into one of the Twelve. Right after the last bite, the best bite, Satan entered. Right after the ceremonial toast, the kiss and hug, Satan entered. It is possible, though not excusable, to understand how this could have occurred "before the sop." Had there been no physical edification, no emotional identification, no spiritual fortification, one could be inclined to understand Judas's feeble, weakened condition.

We all are vulnerable to the wiles of the wicked one before we receive power. We all are vulnerable before salvation, before baptism, before consecration, or before ordination. We are certainly struggling before worship, before prayer meeting, before holy Communion, before fasting, before being anointed with oil, before receiving a word of knowledge, or before a prophetic utterance. We were weak and heavy laden before, but after? Immediately following, straightway, without missing a beat, Satan entered into Judas.

What ought to be alarming is that Satan sneaks in on us. He does not attack with a frontal assault, or even a backdoor barrage; he slips in a side window. When and where we least expect it, at the worse possible time, when the armor is off, the guard is down, and when expectations of us are at an all-time high, it is then that we fall short.

A young man was being considered for the position of executive vice president by the board of directors of a Fortune 500 company. The issue of his compensation was complicated, and the deliberations went long into the morning. The board decided to adjourn for lunch and vote on his selection immediately upon their return. While in the company cafeteria, a member of the board was standing behind the candidate as he went through the food line. He observed the candidate lift his plate and slide a pat of butter under it in an effort to avoid detection by the cashier. When the meeting reconvened, the board member stood, shared what he had just observed, and queried, "If we can't trust him with a three-cent pat of butter, how can we place the company in his hands?"

That candidate missed a golden opportunity because of an

unguarded moment. He traded a three-million dollar compensation package for a three-cent pat of butter. What a trade-off! Have you stopped to calculate some of your losses lately?

We now come to the real danger of an unguarded moment. It is not in having the moment, because such moments are common to us all. Romans 3:23 reminds the critics, "All have sinned, and come short of the glory of God."

Judas excused himself from the table and went out (John 13:30). He went out, went away, and went down. He followed the devilish design of unguarded moments, for they are crafted to place a wedge between your soul and the Savior. If only Judas had confessed his conflict. If only he had had a little talk with Jesus, and told the Savior all about his struggles; Jesus would have heard his faintest cry, and answered by and by.

If only Judas had learned from David, who when confronted with the details of his dalliance with his neighbor's wife, prayed, "Have mercy upon me, O God, according to thy lovingkindness: according unto the multitude of thy tender mercies blot out my transgressions" (Psalm 51:1).

If only Judas had stayed close to Peter, who after his moment of denial, bitterly wept and went into seclusion until summoned by the Savior (Mark 14:72; 16:7). The next time we see Peter he had gone fishing, but by then he was leaving his catch for Christ.

Unfortunately, Judas did not understand that when we are in trouble, we ought run to God, not from God. When we have lost our guard, that is when we need our Guide—the One who specializes in fixing what is broken, making right what is wrong, and adding favor to failure. Call on the One who specializes in wiping tears from our eyes, shame from our souls, burdens from our backs, and worry from our brows. When you lose control, surrender control. Not to the destroyer, but to the Restorer.

Guide me O thou Great Jehovah,
  Pilgrim through this barren land,
I am weak but thou art mighty,
  hold me with thy powerful hand. [2]

Our fervent prayer to the Lord must be,
Hear me, when I cry.
Heal me, when I hurt.
Hide me, when I fail.
Hold me, lest I flee.
Help me, lest I fall.
Feed me.
Fix me.
Fill me, with thy Spirit.

Oh yes, we have our unguarded moments, but instead of turning away with our tear-stained cheeks, let us turn to the Lord and join with the sister who wrote:

I am Thine, O Lord, I have heard Thy voice,
   And it told Thy love to me;
But I long to rise in the arms of faith,
   and be drawn closer to Thee.

Consecrate me now to thy service, Lord,
   By the power of grace divine;
Let my soul look up with a steadfast hope,
   And my will be lost in Thine.

Draw me nearer, nearer, nearer, blessed Lord,
   to the cross where Thou hast died;
Draw me nearer, nearer, nearer, blessed Lord,
   to Thy precious bleeding side.[3]

NOTES

1. "Come Ye Disconsolate," lyrics by Thomas Moore. Public domain.
2. "Guide Me, O Thou Great Jehovah," lyrics by William Williams. Public domain.
3. "I Am Thine, O Lord," lyrics by Fannie J. Crosby. Public domain.

15

MISSING THE MOMENT, MISSING THE BLESSING

WALTER S. THOMAS

MATTHEW 17:10-13, NIV

We would have to admit that we are highly impressed by the accomplishments of some persons. Bill Gates revolutionized the world as we know it with his computer wizardry, and in the process became a billionaire before he was forty years old. Donald Trump, even amid the problems in his personal life, took the stodgy image of real estate acquisition and made it the belle of the financial ball. Kobe Bryant left high school to become a Los Angeles Laker, and even before he reaches age twenty-five, his salary exceeds our wildest imagination. Tiger Woods, who has not seen his thirtieth birthday, has become a legend in his own time and already is compared with the greats in other fields. Martin King was in his late twenties when he surfaced as a national leader of civil rights. In fact, he accomplished feats of record before reaching his thirty-ninth birthday. We need not go far. Even in our town, we have doctors like Levi Watkins and Ben Carson, whose names were of the household variety even before their star had fully risen in the sky. I must admit that I marvel at young rappers and musical artists whose CDs go double platinum and whose contracts yield them tremendous returns, but whose lyrics are even harder to comprehend than the profits they generate. Somehow, whether we like it or not, these persons have been positioned, and in the words of our parents, they were in the right place at the right time. They have seized their moment and stretched for the prize they knew could be theirs.

There are persons, some even our friends, who seem to be able to catch the comet, leap on the star, and grab the bull by the horns. They somehow have what it takes to make it to the next level, whatever that level seems to be. In their home lives, they move forward; on their jobs, they move forward; in their relationship to God, they move forward. They can be compared to Midas of Greek mythology—everything they touch turns to gold. They are the people with whom we started, the persons who joined when we did, the others who came alongside us, and yet they seem to have moved into the stratosphere of life.

Tiger plays golf, Ben Carson performs surgery, Kobe plays ball, Bill Gates engineers the future, Donald Trump presides over a conglomerate, and Martin King led a social revolution in the name of God. I sometimes wonder where the world would be without persons like these—people who make a tremendous difference in life because of what they believe, accept, and do. Where would we have been without the daring of a Charles Drew, the writing of a Daniel Walker, the conviction of a John Brown, the diligence of a Hosea Williams, and the skillful entertainment of a Michael Jordan?

Although I have lifted names that seem to be in the highest of orbits, there are others, many of them close to us, whose contributions were timed and placed in our paths at just the right time. Where would I have been if that sixth-grade teacher had not gone out on a limb for me to go to a different school? What might have been your lot if you had not sent in that application for college or for a mortgage, even though you knew you did not have the resources necessary to bring it to fruition? Somebody had to seize the moment and launch out in some really deep water on your behalf.

One would think that the testimony of the church and its million saints would be an echo of this reality. When we consider who has our backs, who guides our steps, and who has prepared the table for us, it is naturally assumed that we, too, are walking into the days of marvelous blessing and the times of major witness. We are called to be the head and not the tail; yet when we check the record, more often than not, like the last bull rally of the stock market, we miss our moment and fail to advance the kingdom of God. The church collectively misses its moment, and the saints in particular miss their moments. We miss our moments, and we miss our blessings.

I have come to realize that into every transition, God has built a megablessing. In every moment of decision, God has determined results that push forward the Kingdom. God is behind us, and God is pushing us. Where would the church be if we had responded positively to every one of God's "pushes"? The world would be closer to the rapture, and sinners would have left the army of the adversary and thrown themselves into the service of the Lord. If we had responded to every call, racism would have been squashed, sexism banished, and classism put forever aside. If we had responded, young lives would have been saved and old lives made whole, families would have been stabilized, and healing would have been the answer to disease. If you and I had seized the moment in our personal lives and believed . . . I do not need to run that litany. Somehow we—the saved, the called, and the elect of God—have missed our moments. We made the mistake once, but we need to make sure we kill the practice in the future.

I happened upon this reality while reading the story of the Transfiguration. The Master went high up in a mountain to pray and took Peter, James, and John with him. I do not know why the others were not there. Maybe they did not feel like going. Maybe Jesus went too early in the morning and they were still asleep. Maybe they were busy doing other things, or maybe Jesus simply did not ask the others to accompany him. I do not know why they were not there, but Peter, James, and John were. Sometimes we can become so obsessed with reasons why others act the way they do that we miss opportunities. These three were there and that is all that matters. The Bible tells us in Matthew 17:1-3 (NIV):

> After six days Jesus took with him Peter, James and John the brother of James, and led them up a high mountain by themselves. There he was transfigured before them. His face shone like the sun, and his clothes became as white as the light. Just then there appeared before them Moses and Elijah, talking with Jesus.

He was, as the Scriptures declare, transfigured. His face shone and his clothes were radiant. In the first reading of the text, much can be missed that is essential to the moment and to the conversation that will later ensue. Matthew says the Master took Peter, James, and John with him, and that is important. The wording here is intended to convey the fact that they did not just go along. He purposed that these three would be with him. He wanted them to have this experience. Sometimes we have to understand that God wants certain experiences to be a part of our journey, though they will make sense to us later.

When they arrived at the mountaintop, the Lord was transfigured before their eyes. The word for transfigured is our word for metamorphosis. It means a deep and inner change. The text seems to imply that the transfiguration made the Master's clothes shine and his face bright, but that is not what the word means. When this word *metamorphous* is used, the change is in the essence of the object. Its essential nature has changed, like a caterpillar changes into a butterfly. The change was so awesome that the outer garments reflected the inner change. The transfiguration revealed to them the true essence of the one they called Jesus. They were now seeing him in his glory and seeing his splendor. So great was the transfiguration that it also caused his raiment to go through the change. To the world, he was just a carpenter from Nazareth; but on that mountain they saw what human eyes had never beheld. They saw what God had sent to them, the revelation that was in their midst but that they previously had not comprehended.

Joining the Master in the form that was his from the beginning were Moses and Elijah. The disciples were seeing the plan of God and the work of God unfold before their eyes. The Master intended for them to see it. This was his plan! I am so grateful for the things that God intended for me to see. I never would have known them, but he exposed me to them. I have seen his wonders, his grace, his mercy, his love, his understanding, his compassion, his faithfulness, and even his glory. He intended for me to see it. He has done the same for you.

God then spoke and declared, "This is my Son, whom I love; with him I am well pleased. Listen to him!" (Matthew 17:5). In other words, God said, "What you are seeing is really my son. Infused in the fabric of his humanity is the presence and essence of God. Now listen to him. Now that you know who he is, listen to him."

I have no doubt that the disciples were in absolute awe. They had no words, they could make no comment; for when ecstasy has been experienced, language is a poor attendant. Yet, the Master gave them a command that must have seemed impossible. "Tell no one about this!" How could they keep this a secret? How could they keep silent in the marketplace where Jesus was the daily subject of conjecture? How could they not tell the other nine? Why should they not tell it, when all of Judaism was looking for the coming of the messiah and the coming of Elijah would herald his arrival? In fact, they raised that very question to the Master. "Why then do the teachers of the law say that Elijah must come first?" (Matthew 17:10).

And he replied that the Scriptures are true that Elijah must come first, then the messiah would come and erect his kingdom, and of his kingdom there would be no end. The new age would indeed begin. The messiah would be among his people. They were absolutely right about the coming of Elijah and what that meant for the next move of history. Elijah would herald the start of something big. I am sure their eyes stretched wide as they thought with anticipation of what was on the horizon. But then the Master threw a monkey wrench into the machinery of their thinking. He said, in Matthew 17:12, "But I tell you, Elijah has already come, and they did not recognize him, but have done to him everything they wished. In the same way the Son of Man is going to suffer at their hands."

Elijah had come already, not just on that mountain but into their experience, but they not only did not know him, they did not receive! They knew he was talking about John the Baptist.

Had they received John and welcomed his ministry among them, things might have been different. Instead of the cross that was waiting for him in Jerusalem, maybe Jesus would have worn a crown. Instead John was beheaded and the Master's headdress was a crown of thorns. The people of that day, the people of God, Jehovah's children, the sons and daughters of Abraham, had missed their moment and missed their blessing. God's new age could have begun and their oppression could have ceased; instead they were marching down a mountain and headed for a confrontation.

I am preaching this message because the church cannot afford to miss another moment. We play catch up so much, causing the world to miss the splendor and the regality of our God. We are to move this world in God's direction! Too many of us are missing our moments and missing God's moment. We are missing *Kairos*, God's time, and all that is prepared for us; and instead of marching forward, we are crying at our rest stops. It is time to move! God told Moses to tell the children of Israel that they had stayed at the mountain too long, and it was time to take their journey. Some of us have been at our mountains too long, and we have not moved forward. We are waiting on something to come and give us the command. We are waiting on Elijah to tell us to start that ministry, witness to that person, buy that house, stretch on for that job, try something different with those children, believe that we can make it and do it. We are waiting on Elijah, that certainty that will verify the appropriateness of our course. There is just one problem—Elijah has come already!

Now if you missed him the first time, I am preaching this message so that you do not miss him again. God has sent what he is sending but we missed it looking for something else. We cannot afford to miss our moments.

I must admit that I wanted to know why they missed Elijah (Matthew 17:12). I wanted to know how they missed the moment so that I would not duplicate their mistake. They missed their moment and their mighty blessing all because they questioned the packaging! John was almost a wild man. He dressed in camel's hair and ate locusts and wild honey. His style was abrupt and pointed. He cut to the heart of the matter. John decried their lifestyles and did not look like a "glorified Elijah." He looked and acted like someone who had come to do anything but herald a new kingdom. He did not fit the image that they had of Elijah in a glorified state. John just did not look the part! Granted, Elijah was rustic and curt, but centuries of remembering had bathed his reputation and dressed him in the saintly garb of one come to herald the kingdom. They did not recognize him because of the packaging. They were looking for one thing, but God sent another. They were convinced that they knew what and how God was going to act, but they were wrong. It never crossed their minds that Elijah was a sign, and that John was operating in their day and age as Elijah. They were straitjacketed in their thinking, and therefore, missed their moment and their blessing.

This is precisely what the Master was trying to show the disciples on the Mount of Transfiguration. To understand what God was doing, and the task to which they had been called, they needed to look behind the mask of the physical, the temporal, and even the intellectual, and see the glory of God that was being revealed. The disciples had not seen the inner essence of Jesus. They had been with the Teacher for three years and understood him as Prophet, Teacher, and even Son of God. They marveled at his wisdom, and were amazed at his miracle-working power, but still they missed the essence of who he really was! They knew him as Messiah, but they had preconceived notions about the promised one and Jesus did not fit. The world was going to miss the messiah because they missed the messenger.

We miss our moments because we, too, are looking for the wrong thing! We miss the major move of God because we have missed the transition before the move. We miss the place of blessing because we have missed the transition to that blessing. John was the transition, the herald, the announcer, but they missed the announcement, and therefore, the presentation. They did not understand that God was moving and revealing his move through John. And when the move came to fulfillment in Jesus, they missed that, too. Would to God that this did not have to repeat itself in our lives, but that does not seem to be the case. God moves, and we miss it because divine movement often is not packaged in a way that we can accept based on what we expect. You see, it is our expectations that get in the way of our blessings. We have expectations about people, things, and situations that block the way that God wants to deal with us. We have to have certain people in our lives. We have to work on certain jobs. We have to live in a certain neighborhood. Yet often God moves in a mysterious way. The Lord does not come in the manner that we expect, yet still is moving on our behalf. We miss our moment waiting on things to be a certain way.

I am convinced that this is why so many people still miss Christ. He is not packaged the way they think he is to be. He does not wear the garments of a royal leader. His parents are peasants. His ministry ends with a death on a cross. How can someone follow a man who meets with this kind of fate? The answer is simple. They can follow him because he is the Christ. The transfiguration revealed that things like clothing and ancestry were just the human covering. The essence of his being was the essence of God. He came the way he did so that he could show us the potential in us. On the mount, he revealed the image of God; and it is the same image that is in and on each of us.

Spiritual things do not come neatly gift-wrapped all the time. Sometimes they come in the paper bags of rough situations, or the cardboard boxes of difficult moments; but nonetheless, they come our way and we must look beyond the packaging and see what God is offering. We all can boast of moments when God moved beyond our skepticism to bless us beyond our belief. He did it, and we were made better. Had we held to the packaging, we would have missed our blessings. The packaging almost caused us to miss some of our greatest blessings. Maybe we almost missed the job because of the drive to get there. Perhaps we almost missed the house because of cars on the street. Or we almost missed the school experience because of the way that the dormitory looked. Maybe we nearly missed the quality relationship because the packaging was not perfect. We almost missed the blessing of a quality church home because of the packaging. We looked at its size, its music, or its location; but there comes a moment when the packaging must take a back seat to the perfecting!

The people missed John because they wanted the packaging to be a certain way; and in the process, they missed being perfected. We must not be so consumed with the package that we fail to let God work on us and accomplish God's will. I am so glad that I did not miss my moment in coming to this church. I had a vision of what the pastor's office should look like, and the one I had was as far from that as east is from west. Yet, I put the packaging behind and saw Elijah, God's announcement and transition, and I was ready to see the next powerful divine move. I want to repeat this truth. There is always a transition between where a person is and where that person is going. Into that transition, God sends an Elijah. Now, Elijah may be a person or an idea, but if you miss your Elijah, the chances are better than good that you also will miss the next major move. You see, it, too, will come to you disguised. We have to take time learning to understand what God is saying and doing. We must learn to interpret divine actions.

John had been in their midst preaching in the Jordan River, yet they never made the connection between his message and the coming of Elijah. Moreover, they misunderstood what Elijah would do and, therefore, missed the moment of the visitation. They knew the Messiah would come and set the kingdom back on its proper footing. He would return the golden age. It would be Elijah's job to announce this coming and also to prepare the nation. He would set their minds back to the Word of God. They were looking for someone who would announce that soon the Roman regime would be expelled. They looked for someone who would, in priestly words, call them back to God. Yet John was anything but this. He did not address the Romans, nor did he make pliable his contempt for their godless living. The prophet Elijah addressed his invectives to the kings and leaders, but John the Baptist took on everyone, crying but one word, "Repent!" The Jews were clear that the Gentiles were heathens and pagans; but John let them know that they were no better. The Jewish authorities also needed to clean up their act and get their house in order. For many, this was unthinkable and definitely unbelievable.

At this point, I understood why they did not see John as the Elijah, and why they missed their moment. They could not accept what John was saying. They could not surrender their previous position! We miss the moment. We cannot stand to hear the voice of self-correction. We cannot see the fault in our own lives. Yet, we never get to the fullness of the blessings that are on the next level without looking at ourselves and realizing that there must be some correction. We have to be changed before we can live in the moment that God has prepared for us. It is a rebellious spirit that causes us to turn away from the voice of self-correction. We would rather be hurt, we would rather become angry, but the truth is that we cannot seize the moment without certain changes happening in us.

The words of John may sting, but the sting is not that of a viper with venom that will kill; it is the prick of a needle that injects healing serum into our bodies. In order to grow, we must shed. We must adapt and learn to reinterpret. Early scientists thought the world was flat, but Galileo discovered that the world was indeed round. Had civilization clung to that erroneous notion, everything we understand would have been affected. One idea must be allowed to birth another. The Gentiles were not the only ones living outside the will of God; the Jews were, too. Let me make this powerful assertion. Whenever you start doing self-evaluation and introspection that has as its aim growing and becoming, get ready, because you are about to both see and enter a new moment of divine appointment. Had they been able to hear John, they would have been ready to receive what God was about to send.

This is a message for the church. So often we mistakenly believe that we are right, and that it is the world that needs correction. We fail to realize that we have areas of exposure that make us worse than those outside the Kingdom's walls. We see the flaws in others, but shy away from addressing the faults that lie within our gates. We have to watch our attitudes and our behaviors. We have to look at what we say and what we do. We have to see that there are areas where we need work. Too many churches miss their moment because they are too busy criticizing what others are doing while failing to look closely at themselves. Jesus cautioned against specializing in pulling the mote out of another's eye when there is a two-by-four hanging in front of one's own head. We must hear a message that causes us to see ourselves and, in so doing, respond positively to what "Elijah" has shared with us.

They missed their moment. God was about to do something mega in their lives and they missed it. They absolutely missed it. The Lord sent the forerunner to announce that it was about to happen, and they missed it. They missed a great blessing. Why did they miss it? They missed it because they were looking for a different packaging. They missed it because they could not let go of previously held positions. They missed the moment because they were not spiritually ready to receive it! Look at what the Book says:

> "But I tell you, Elijah has already come, and they did not recognize him, but have done to him everything they wished. In the same way the Son of Man is going to suffer at their hands." Then the disciples understood that he was talking to them about John the Baptist.

They were not spiritually in line with what God was doing so they missed the moment that God had prepared. You see, in order to receive your moment, you have to become spiritually prepared. Too many of us are simply worldly prepared. We know our three Rs, and we have mastered our academic studies; but we have not invested time in our spiritual studies. The time has come for the people of God to become students of the Word and disciples of the Spirit. We have to start making time for prayer and for the things of the Spirit. Moreover, we have to say to ourselves that knowing God is our utmost priority. You see, God has some unique ways of moving; and if we have not cultivated our spiritual understanding, then we will not understand divine activity in our lives. The apostle Paul told the Corinthian church, "The man without the Spirit does not accept the things that come from the Spirit of God, for they are foolishness to him, and he cannot understand them, because they are spiritually discerned" (1 Corinthians 2:14).

It takes the Spirit of God to comprehend divine movement. Elijah realized that unless we are attuned we will miss it.

> The LORD said, "Go out and stand on the mountain in the presence of the LORD, for the LORD is about to pass by." Then a great and powerful wind tore the mountains apart and shattered the rocks before the LORD, but the LORD was not in the wind. After the wind there was an earthquake, but

the LORD was not in the earthquake. After the earthquake came a fire, but the LORD was not in the fire. And after the fire came a gentle whisper. When Elijah heard it, he pulled his cloak over his face and went out and stood at the mouth of the cave. (1 Kings 19:11-13)

It was the Spirit that made Elijah aware. The packaging might have fooled him, but because he had cultivated a spiritual life, he knew the still small voice. Our community may miss the moment because we are not spiritually prepared. We have to spend more time understanding and knowing the God who called cosmos out of chaos. You see, the better we understand our Creator, the better we understand how God operates, and how God operates through us. That is the mandate. Be ready for the moment by being ready for God!

We need to be able to recognize the voice and see the signs. We need to work at walking with the Lord so that we can seize the moment and be blessed. I must confess that I do not want to miss my blessing; I have been through too much already. I want to be able to lay hands on what God has put into my life. I want to know God, to understand God's ways, and to be ready for God's next move. I have seen some powerful moves of the Spirit already, and I must admit they have blown my mind. I do not want to miss the next one! I am praying more and seeking the Lord more. I am listening more, and letting God guide me more. I am reading more and believing more. I know that God is moving in our midst, and I want to see the transition and be ready for the fullness. Our forebears put it best, "None but the righteous shall see God."

I close by emphasizing, *Do not miss it because it is too valuable and it has been prepared for you.* The world missed the Jesus moment, but thank God there were some who had grown spiritual enough to realize that he was too powerful to have been destroyed on that cross. They gave up their ideas about the power of death and followed women to an empty tomb. They sought his face in the Word in that upper room; and on

Pentecost, the power fell down on them. They were ready, and God was working. Do not miss the Jesus move! He is moving right now. He is knocking on doors offering salvation and pouring the power of his spirit. He is changing lives and creating wholeness. He is establishing relationships and reaffirming his Father's love. Don't miss it, because it is all just for you.

16
FINDING THE HAND OF GOD

RALPH DOUGLAS WEST

MATTHEW 14:29-30, NIV

Theologian R.C. Sproul has written a book entitled *The Invisible Hand*.[1] In it, Sproul endeavors to answer the question: "Do all things really work for good?" He attempts to answer the question theologically, from a word that practically has been dismissed from Christian vernacular, *providence*. For providence speaks of the acts of God, that there is nothing that comes to our lives, accidentally or coincidentally, that does not pass through the approving hands of God first. So when we think of providence in those terms, we also conclude that not only is God acting in our lives, but God is looking after our lives. The reading of history will help us sense and recognize the different times when God has acted on our behalf, and the other times when God has looked after our lives.

William Cowper, a hymnist in the eighteenth century, has a fascinating history. He has given birth to more than sixty-nine hymns, all of them born out of pain predicaments. You see, William Cowper was born to an English clergyman in the 1700s who was married to a woman of nobility. Cowper was reared in a family of devout religion and Christian faith, but at the age of six, Cowper's mother died. Later in life, he would comment that not one day had gone by that he had not mourned the death of his mother. As he matured, his father encouraged him to study

law. He was an excellent law student; but on the day of his examination to stand before the bar, the weight of the examination
was so strenuous that he suffered a mental breakdown. That
same night Cowper attempted suicide.

Because of his frail physical and emotional condition, his
daddy admitted him into an insane asylum where he was diag-
nosed as suffering from melancholy. After eighteen months in
that asylum, Cowper read Romans 3:25. When he saw that the
blood of Jesus Christ was available for the propitiation of sin, he
developed a relationship with the Lord Jesus. But his days never
lightened; they were still dark. He attempted suicide on another
occasion. Dark, deep moments of melancholic depression
became so prevalent in the life of William Cowper that the only
out he could find was to try and take his own life. After finding
this relationship with God, you would think that peace would
come to his life; but he was always dogged by melancholy, the
loss of his mother, depression, and frustration. He was always in
difficulty.

Up until the time of his death, William Cowper believed that
somehow God would not accept him into the kingdom. Then on
his deathbed, Cowper lifted his eyes and saw the face of God;
only then was he able to say, "Now, I know that God is not
ashamed of me, and God will not cast me out."

But William Cowper leaves something for us to sing in
moments of dark, deep melancholic difficulties. He left this
hymn for us, and it would do you well to sing it in moments of
your own difficulty:

> O God, in a mysterious way,
> Great wonders You perform.
> You plant Your footsteps in the sea
> And ride upon the storm. [2]

You see, although his life was dogged by difficulties, at the
moment of death William Cowper finally came to know that the

invisible hand of God was acting on his behalf and had been looking after him all of his life.

We come because we, too, know that there are times when we misread the hand of God—those moments when God would be there, or so we have been taught, and it appeared that God was not. In our own folklore, we have often heard: God may not come when you want him; but whenever he arrives, he's always on time.

We espouse this thought, yet we ask the question, "If God is on time, then what is the delay?" And so the story in Matthew 14 helps us to understand the timing of God during those moments of difficulty; that in our difficulties, God is always there to deliver us. Do not forget that there are moments in our lives when the unseen hand of God cannot be traced. We cannot feel God . . . we do not see God. It is almost as if we cannot experience God, but the Lord is always there.

Beginning with verse 22 in Matthew 14, the order of the story goes as follows. Jesus dismissed his disciples after they had satisfied the hungry stomachs of the crowd. According to John's interpretation of this event, the people in the crowd wanted to crown Christ prematurely. Stepping away from these attempts, Jesus dismissed his disciples. He also instructed them to get into a boat and go to the west side of the shore. He would meet them on that side a little later. He disassociated himself from the crowd, and alone, isolated, and in contemplation with God on a mountain, he entered deep and protracted prayer. Mark tells the same story in chapter 6 and he adds a strange twist to the telling of the story.

The story happens on a clear night, around six o'clock p.m. It was a nautical dream. You could see the constellations against the sky. The moon was like a big, beautiful pearl positioned against black velvet. The waters were glassy and still, no whitecaps out on the sea. The night was a navigator's dream, the perfect sailing weather. The disciples got into the boat without a word of resistance. No saying, "We'll wait until you're ready." As they set out, however, something happened. The dream sky changed. The moon was lost behind the clouds. No star could be seen. The waves rose twelve to fifteen feet high. The winds blew the boat from one side to the other. The bow of the ship was dipping in the water, taking on water. Panic and terror could be seen in the faces of the disciples. These Christ followers, with their eyes bulging out of their heads, gripped the oars as they tried to row through the night. Yet while they were rowing, the unseen God saw them.

We must not miss this important truth. If you are rowing against life, and the winds are pushing you back, and you find yourself in difficulty, the first thing you need to know is that you can expect God to come to you during your moments of difficulty. The narrative in the Gospel of Mark slips in this phrase, that they were "straining at the oars, because the wind was against them" (Mark 6:48, NIV), and the words imply that they were torturously rowing—that their hands were on the oars and their knuckles were whitening with their effort and their fear, and the cool stinging mist of the waters was making it almost unbearable; but they kept on rowing.

So the question then comes: "What was Jesus doing while they were rowing?" Well, the answer is, "He was praying." But the flip question for each of his disciples is, "If Jesus is praying, what are we to be doing?" The answer is "rowing." However you look at it, you have to do what you have been commanded to do. Obedience works that way. Without a word of discrepancy, the Twelve got in the boat, and they went on their way in the direction that Jesus, the Captain, had told them to go.

But is not obedience supposed to birth peace? I mean, we have been told "If you're obedient, then good things will come your way." But then there is that question again: "Do things really work together for the good of those of us who love God?" We have been taught that if you obey, peace will come. But if you are a conscientious Christian, you have to at least smirk at that statement; because you know that most of your difficulty has come not when you have done something wrong but when you have done the right thing.

Difficulty often comes our way when we have done the right thing. It is one thing to toil in difficulty because we've done the wrong thing; then we at least can feel like our toiling is a discipline or punishment for our errors. But to suffer when we are doing right seems so paradoxical.

God has told you, "Get on the boat," and you didn't negotiate. He commanded, "Meet me on the west side."

You responded, "I'm going." And when you started off in life, the skies were clear. There was not a cloud to be found; the water was glassy still. But no sooner than you did what God said, all chaos broke out . . . winds everywhere . . . just storms everywhere. And while the storm is raging in your life, you are asking the question: "Where in the world is God? If I'm in this with God, where is God?"

What we all need to know is that even though the unseen God may not seem present, God sees! In other words, even when you cannot see God, God sees you.

When my son, Ralph, was a boy, I took him to Toys-R-Us, and he got detached from me. Ralph being my first child, my fatherly instincts caused me to panic. Yet, because I could see the doors, I knew that he had not exited them. He was fumbling around with some gadgets I supposed, but I could not find him. Up one corridor, I paced, and down another . . . around a corridor . . . around another aisle . . . peeping . . . looking to find him amid a crowd of people in the Christmas rush; but I could not find my son. I found a security guard and I asked him, "Do you have surveillance in the store?"

He said, "Yes."

I then asked, "Do you have a monitor?"

"Yes."

"Can I look at the monitor?"

"Yes."

"Can you scan the floor?"

"Yes."

The guard began to scan up and down the aisles, and there I saw my son playing with toys, but he was clearly in a state of panic. Maybe he was trying to find comfort in playing until I found him. My son was all by himself among people he did not know. Our first child was feeling lost and alone, and I did not know what to do. I asked the guard, "Do you have an intercom?" He said, "Yes."

I said, "Keep the camera on him." Then I got on the intercom and said, "Ralph." My son looked around because he recognized my voice. I continued, "Stay where you are." He started looking around him. "It's Daddy," I said. "Don't move. I see you although you can't see me. Stay where you are."

In those moments, when you think that God cannot see you or that you cannot see God, always remember that God sees you. The invisible hand of God is active and is looking after your life.

There the disciples were, from six o'clock to midnight, six hours toiling, and then from midnight to three a.m., they toiled some more. John records that in that nine hour period they had rowed only four miles; for every time they rowed forward, the wind would push them backward. They kept rowing, and in the fourth watch, between three a.m. and six a.m., Jesus came toward them, walking on the water! I don't want to move too soon.

He came at the fourth watch, but why not sooner? Does it not seem like ten o'clock at night was just as good as three o'clock in the morning? Why not sooner? If God sees me struggling in the storm, why does deliverance not come sooner? Why leave me out there? Well, the answer is simple: I do not know.

I do not know why the Lord does not come any sooner.

I do not know why God does not come until the bank account is empty.

I do not know why God does not grant some healing until the other side of eternity.

I do not know why the Lord decides to give comfort after the body has been placed in the ground.

I do not know why God decides to lift you up only after you have fallen down many times; but I have a suggestion. It just might be that God knows that it is stress and struggle that give you strength, and that if divine aid comes too soon, you will not become what God has intended.

Do you know about the emperor butterfly? The emperor butterfly, after it has gone through its various development stages, begins to break out of its cocoon. As it pushes through, the insect strains because the hole in the cocoon is smaller than the butterfly. But it pushes and pushes . . . and it is painful . . . and it is a struggle.

One time, a little boy was looking at this natural process of pushing and the struggling, and the painful efforts of this butterfly trying to get out of the cocoon. In a darkroom, the boy watched this beautiful butterfly pushing, straining, wiggling, trying to exit the cocoon until he could see the insect's pulsating body. After watching this for a while, the boy decided he would help. Carefully he picked up the cocoon, took out his knife and just slit the hole a little in the cocoon so that the butterfly would not have to struggle so much. Well, the insect did not struggle nearly as much after receiving help from human hands; but something interesting had happened. When the butterfly got out of the cocoon, it was still beautiful; however, it could not fly. The pushing, and straining, and pain sends blood into the butterfly's veins to develop its wings so that when the butterfly comes out of the cocoon, it is able to fly.

There are moments when God sees you pushing, straining, struggling, and trying to get out. Cutting a hole would make things easier, but you will not fly! Sometimes God has had to let you push, strain, and struggle so, when you come out, you can celebrate the pushing, straining, and struggling. But while you are pushing, straining, and struggling, just remember that God sees you while you are pushing. God is watching you struggle, and is there to protect you if anything were to happen.

Well, this God of ours can be expected to come in our moments of difficulty, but the text is tailored to tell us something else. Not only can we expect God to come in moments of difficulty, but we can experience God's deliverance during the moment of difficulty. God comes during the fourth watch of the night walking out on the water; water-walking is preserved for God only. Water-walking belongs to God alone. I guess God can walk on it since it is a divine creation! Water would not be if God did not say, "Let it be." Our God is the God on the water.

When God comes walking on the water, God's divinity and deity are revealed out on that water. But, there is a note of caution. When God comes out on the water, do not fail to identify the Lord. When God comes to our deliverance, many of us miss the moment because divine assistance does not come the way that we expect.

You have to keep looking at the story. When Jesus came out of the water, the disciples were terrified because they thought he was a ghost. They thought he was a fantasy. They thought he was an apparition. They thought he was some other ungod coming out on the water, so they screamed: "It's a ghost!" They did not recognize him.

The problem with many of us is that when God comes to us, we are looking for God at a certain time, in a certain way, and in a certain place. But we cannot nail God down. We cannot domesticate God, the divine Mover. God can move any way that God wants to move. God can come at any time God wants to come; and yet they missed God.

Did you catch that? How many times have we missed God when God has been speaking to us? We were looking for the answer, and God said, "You've got my Word." How many times have we needed God's comfort, and someone has come by and put big, loving arms of encouragement around us? How often have we said, "If there is a God, show yourself," and then the sun gets up in the morning and settles in the evening? How many times have we felt a gentle breeze speaking the name of God?

If you are looking for God, just look around. God is all over the place. You cannot miss God if you are looking; yet fear can blind you and cause you to miss God's arrival. You will miss God, and many folks have done it—missed God's appearance in the fourth watch of the night, speaking one word, "Be not afraid" (Mark 6:50, KJV). These are words of affirmation, "It is I," Jesus said, speaking words of identification. Jesus says, "Be of good cheer. It is I; be not afraid," speaking words of consolation.

When the disciples heard the voice saying, "It is I," that should have been enough to convince them. Peter said, "Lord, if it be you, stop." This is in Matthew's Gospel. The purpose of the Gospel of Matthew is the identification of the king of a Jewish world. In Matthew 4, there is a strange vernacular used in protesting the identification of Jesus. It is the same speech vernacular that Peter uses in Matthew 14. For when Jesus says, "It is I . . . ." Peter said, "If it be . . . ."

In Matthew 4, Satan said, "If it be . . . ." Could it be that in this text Peter never had to come out on the water because God's identity would be proven? For it seems like the identification "It is I . . . " ought to be enough. For who else could walk on water? Nowhere in history has the enemy of God performed such a feat! So, it seems to me that "It is I" ought to be enough; yet Peter said, "But if it be . . . ."

Satan said, "But if you be . . . turn stone to bread." Peter said, "If you be . . . let me walk out on water." Both seemed to be treading in territory that did not belong to them, and there Jesus is. The text does not raise questions on the identity of Jesus, but rather on how we recognize him. I conclude that "It is I" ought to be enough; but it seems that when Satan raised the question, he was testing Jesus. When Peter raised the question, he was doubting Jesus.

Peter proposed, "If you be . . . ," and Jesus said, "Come on! I'm looking for some water walkers. I'm looking for somebody who will get out of the boat and get away from ordinary living. If you want to walk with me, come on."

And Peter got out on the water and walked. While walking, he heard the voice of the wind. And when he heard it—let me stop right here—because when he walked, he was looking at the object of his faith. When he started sinking, he had taken his vision off of the One who could sustain him. And if you are going to keep steady, you have to keep your eye on that which is stable.

Some of you know about boating. One summer, my wife, Sureta, Joe Ratliff, and his wife, Doris, and I went sailing in the French Polynesian Islands. While we were sailing, ol' Ratliff got sick. Doris tried to help him, but she got sick, too. I laughed because I knew something about sailing that a lot of folks on the boat did not know. Two things you do when sailing in salt water are: first, you drink a little of it; and second you wash your face and hair in it. Some folks who know sailing know what I am talking about. But there is something more important to consider. When you are sailing, and the waves are up twelve to fourteen feet, rocking up and down, you have to find something that is steady and keep your eye on it.

In your times of storm, you've got to keep your eye on Jesus, who is steady, so that when everything else is up and down and bounding, you can maintain your footing. Peter started sinking; but that ain't bad, because if you want to experience the hand of God, there is no time to experience it like when you are sinking. Sink sometime, and God always will be there to hold. Have you ever been there? . . . You've been sinking in life, but God's hand has been there to hold.

One more thing: experience God as a deliverer from difficulty, but do not forget to express gratitude to God for delivering you. Jesus picked Peter up and he walked back to the boat. They got in the boat and the storm stilled. In Matthew 8, Jesus told the storm, "Peace be still." In Mark 6, when Jesus walks on the storm-tossed sea, he did not say a word. He went and got Peter and walked to the boat. They got in the boat, and the storm died. When the storm died, it died immediately—the same way that the storm came. The stars that were lost by the graying clouds returned. They became like candles, and the boat like an altar. The disciples then got on their knees and worshiped Jesus, saying, "You are the Son of God."

You see, the only real expression any of us can have once God has delivered us is to recognize who God is and get on our knees and worship the Lord. That is the only proper response. You have to worship God before you tell the story. If you tell the story before worship, you may begin to think that it was your own nautical maneuvering that got you out of your storm and forget to tell that it was Jesus walking in the fourth watch of the night who came and delivered you.

In Mark's interpretation, when he wrote that they worshiped the Lord, he indicated that they anchored the boat. Now, I don't know if it means anything or not. Mark 6 reads, "When they got to where they were going, they anchored the boat."

Let me close by telling you that the hand of God acts, is active, and is looking after your life. Nothing comes to you accidentally; it comes providentially. It may be negative, it may not be good on the surface; but somewhere, somehow, God has a way of turning

bad into good . . .

negative into positive . . .

minus into plus . . .

darkness into light . . .

sadness into joy . . .

despair into peace . . .

and helplessness into hope.

Whatever anchoring is in the story, it must have some metaphorical connection to what faith is; for not only were they fearful and frightened, they were faithless.

I asked a friend who is a boater, "Man, why do you keep your boat docked like this?" He told me the reasons why. I knew the obvious reasons, but I asked a man who watches over the docks, "What happens to these boats when storms come?" He began to tell me about some plastic containers that they put on the side so that when the water whooshes and the wind hits it, the water won't crack the hull of the ship.

I said, "Uh-huh."

He said, "But preacher, let me tell you where the boat really belongs in a storm." He continued, "Move it from the dock, put it out in the open sea, and drop anchor; because the boat is made to handle the storm and the anchor keeps it from drifting away. "The boat belongs in the storm," the man said, "but if you don't want to lose the boat, anchor deep."

You cannot prevent storms. Storms are inevitable. Obedience will construct the storm; but when you are in the storm, know that God is looking after you. Anchor deep and ride the storm. I have one last thing to tell you. Remember when I asked you what Jesus was doing on the mountain? He was praying, but he was praying a certain prayer. Jesus is praying the prayer that he himself would come to answer, "Save them." So when you anchor deep, know that God will come to answer God's own prayer. That is why we can ride the storm.

In times like these, you need an anchor. In times like these, you need a Savior. Be sure—be very sure that your anchor holds and grips the solid rock. That rock is Jesus. He's the only one. So, anchor deep! Anchor deep! Storms may come—anchor deep! Winds may blow—anchor deep! The treacherous howl may come—anchor deep! But when the storm comes—anchor deep!

NOTES

1. R. C. Sproul, *The Invisible Hand* (Nashville: Word Publishing, 1997).

2. "God Moves in a Mysterious Way," lyrics by William Cowper. Public domain.

CONTRIBUTORS

Claude R. Alexander Jr. has been pastor of University Park Baptist Church in Charlotte, North Carolina for more than ten years.

Ronald D. Barton has served as pastor of Shady Oak Baptist Church in Simpsonville, South Carolina, for more than eleven years.

Charles E. Booth is senior pastor of Mount Olivet Baptist Church in Columbus, Ohio; professor of preaching at Trinity Lutheran Seminary in Columbus; and the founder of the Mount Olivet Christian Academy. Dr. Booth is also an advisory board member of *The African American Pulpit.*

John R. Bryant is the presiding prelate of the fifth episcopal district of the African Methodist Episcopal Church in Dallas, Texas. Dr. Bryant is also author of *God Can: Sermons of Encouragement from the Life of Elijah.*

William H. Curtis is senior pastor of the Mt. Ararat Baptist Church in Pittsburgh, Pennsylvania.

H. Beecher Hicks Jr. is the senior minister of Metropolitan Baptist Church in Washington D.C., and the author of *Preaching Through a Storm* and *Correspondence with a Cripple* *from Tarsus.* Dr. Hicks is also president of Martin Luther King Fellows, Inc., and of Kerygma Associates, a religious consulting service.

Carolyn Ann Knight is founder and president of CAN DO Ministries. Dr. Knight currently serves as chair of the homiletics department at the Interdenominational Theological Center in Atlanta, Georgia, and is an advisory board member of *The African American Pulpit.*

Walter Malone Jr. is founder and pastor of Canaan Missionary Baptist Church in Louisville, Kentucky, and serves as an instructor in the Congress of Christian Education of the National Baptist Convention, U.S.A., Inc. Dr. Malone is the author of two books: *An Operative Faith for Oppressed People* and *From Holy Power to Holy Profit.*

Trinette V. McCray is president of American Baptist Churches, USA for the 2000-2001 biennium. Previously vice president from 1998-1999, she is the first African American woman minister elected to the position. Dr. McCray is campus minister and director of Multicultural Relations at Cardinal Stritch University in Milwaukee, Wisconsin, and serves as an associate minister at Calvary Baptist Church.

Vashti Murphy McKenzie is bishop in the African Methodist Episcopal Church and an advisory board member of *The African American Pulpit.* She is author of *Not Without a Struggle: Leadership Development for African American Women in Ministry.*

Diane Givens Moffett serves as associate pastor of Elmwood United Presbyterian Church in East Orange, New Jersey. Her book of meditations about self-identity for African American Christians is to be published by Judson Press.

Alfred A. Owens Jr. is founder and pastor of the 6,000-member Greater Mt. Calvary Holy Church, located in the heart of Washington, D.C.

James C. Perkins has served nearly two decades as pastor of Greater Christ Baptist church in Detroit, Michigan. He is author of *Building Up Zion's Walls: Ministry for Empowering the African American Family* (Judson Press).

Dennis V. Proctor is the pastor of the Pennsylvania Avenue A.M.E. Zion Church in Baltimore, Maryland. He has been inducted into the Martin Luther King Jr. Board of Preachers at Morehouse College in Atlanta, Georgia. Dr. Proctor is also coauthor of *Christians Under Construction: A Guide to Spiritual Growth*.

Walter S. Thomas is pastor of the New Psalmist Baptist Church in Baltimore, Maryland. Dr. Thomas is also author of *Spiritual Navigation for the 21st Century: Sermons from Walter Thomas* and *Good Meat Makes Its Own Gravy: 135 Servings for the Soul* (both published by Judson Press).

Ralph Douglas West is pastor of the Brookhollow Baptist Church (The Church without Walls) in Dallas, Texas. He is the author of *A Journey Back to Me: Rediscovering Physical, Emotional, and Spiritual Wholeness*.

ADDITIONAL PREACHING RESOURCES

AVAILABLE AT YOUR LOCAL BOOKSTORE OR CALL JUDSON PRESS AT 1-800-458-3766

THE AFRICAN PRESENCE IN THE BIBLE
Gospel Sermons Rooted in History
William D. Watley and Raquel Annette St. Clair

AFROCENTRIC SERMONS
The Beauty of Blackness in the Bible
Kenneth L. Waters Sr.

BEST BLACK SERMONS
Edited by William M. Philpot

A BOLDER PULPIT
Reclaiming the Moral Dimension of Preaching
David P. Gushee and Robert H. Long

BORN TO PREACH
Essays in Honor of the Ministry of Henry and Ella Mitchell
Edited by Samuel K. Roberts

BRING THE FULL TITHE
Sermons on the Grace of Giving
William D. Watley

THE CERTAIN SOUND OF THE TRUMPET
Crafting a Sermon of Authority
Samuel D. Proctor

FIRST-PERSON PREACHING
Bringing New Life to Biblical Stories
Daniel L. Buttry

FROM MESS TO MIRACLE AND OTHER SERMONS
William D. Watley

GOOD NEWS!
Sermons of Hope for Today's Families
Jeremiah A. Wright Jr.; edited by Jini Kilgore Ross

"HOW SHALL THEY HEAR?"
Effective Preaching for Vital Faith
Samuel D. Proctor

INTERPRETING GOD'S WORD IN BLACK PREACHING
Warren H. Stewart Sr.

LIVING WATER FOR THIRSTY SOULS
Unleashing the Power of Exegetical Preaching
Marvin A. McMickle

NO OTHER HELP I KNOW
Sermons on Prayer and Spirituality
Edited by J. Alfred Smith Sr.

OUTSTANDING BLACK SERMONS
Volume 1 – Edited by J. Alfred Smith Sr.
Volume 2 – Edited by Walter B. Hoard
Volume 3 – Edited by Milton E. Owens Jr.

PREACHING IN TWO VOICES
Sermons on the Women in Jesus' Life
William D. Watley and Suzan D. Johnson Cook

PREACHING TO THE BLACK MIDDLE CLASS
Words of Challenge, Words of Hope
Marvin A. McMickle

THE SACRED ART
Preaching and Theology in the African American Tradition
Olin P. Moyd

THE SERMON AS SYMPHONY
Preaching the Literary Forms of the New Testament
Mike Graves

SERMON ON THE MOUNT
Clarence Jordan

SERMONS FROM THE BLACK PULPIT
Samuel D. Proctor and William D. Watley

SERMONS ON SPECIAL DAYS
Preaching through the Year in the Black Church
William D. Watley

SPIRITUAL NAVIGATION FOR THE 21st CENTURY
Sermons from Walter Thomas
Walter S. Thomas; edited by Jean Alicia Elster

THOSE PREACHING WOMEN
Volume 1: Sermons by Black Women Preachers
Volume 2: More Sermons by Black Women Preachers
Volume 3: African American Preachers Tackle Tough Questions
Ella Pearson Mitchell

WHAT MAKES YOU SO STRONG?
Sermons of Joy and Strength from Jeremiah A. Wright, Jr.
Edited by Jini Kilgore Ross

WISDOM OF THE AGES
The Mystique of the African American Preacher
Edited by Robert Johnson-Smith II

WOMEN: TO PREACH OR NOT TO PREACH?
21 Outstanding Black Preachers Say Yes!
Edited by Ella Pearson Mitchell

THE WORDS OF GARDNER TAYLOR
Volume 1: NBC Radio Sermons, 1959–1970
Volume 2: Sermons from the Middle Years, 1970–1980
Volume 3: Quintessential Classics, 1980–Present
Volume 4: Special Occasion and Expository Sermons
Volume 5: Lectures, Essays, and Interviews
Gardner C. Taylor; compiled by Edward L. Taylor

YOU HAVE TO FACE IT TO FIX IT
Sermons on the Challenges of Life
William D. Watley